SEVE:
THE YOUNG CHAMPION

To All Our Friends

SEVE:
THE YOUNG CHAMPION

SEVERIANO BALLESTEROS
AND DUDLEY DOUST

Illustrations by Jim McQueen

Foreword by Lee Trevino

HODDER & STOUGHTON
LONDON   SYDNEY   AUCKLAND   TORONTO

Also by Dudley Doust

THE RETURN OF THE ASHES (with Mike Brearley)
THE ASHES RETAINED (with Mike Brearley)
IAN BOTHAM: THE GREAT ALL-ROUNDER

Photo credits:
First three pages of colour photographs by Phil Sheldon;
page 4 by James Mortimer/*Sunday Times*.
Chris Smith/*Sunday Times*: pages 4–5, 8, 103, 108–9.
Property of Author: pages 10, 11, 12.
Associated Newspapers Group Ltd: pages 14, 15, 127.
Firestone Hispania: page 19.
Phil Sheldon: pages 21, 24, 40 (bottom), 41, 47, 49, 50, 55, 61, 64, 82, 84–5 (centre), 86–7, 94, 106, 107, 124–5, 134, 137, 140–1, 143.
Lester Nehamkin/UNI-Managers International: page 22.
U.M.I.: pages 23, 73, 79.
Peter Dazeley: pages 27, 32, 36 (bottom), 40 (top), 48, 84 (left), 85 (right), 97, 98, 117.
Bert Neale: page 31.
Syndication International: page 34.
Derek Rowe (photos) Ltd: pages 36 (top).
Reportajes Alonso: page 38.
Press Association: pages 44–5, 63, 65, 78.
Peter Chapman: page 56.
Steve Powell/All-Sport; pages 58–9.
David Reed/*Sunday Times*: page 72.
William S. Paton: page 76.
Times Newspapers Ltd: pages 77, 132.
Popperfoto: pages 91, 122–3.
Golf Digest: page 101.
Associated Press: page 114.
James Mortimer/*Sunday Times*: pages 118, 129.

BOOK DESIGN BY BOB HOOK

BRITISH LIBRARY CATALOGUING IN PUBLICATION DATA
DOUST, DUDLEY
SEVE THE YOUNG CHAMPION.
1. BALLESTEROS, SEVERIANO
2. GOLFERS – SPAIN – BIOGRAPHY
I. TIME   II. BALLESTEROS, SEVERIANO
796.352'092'4   GV964.B/

ISBN 0 340 25272 3

CONTENTS

FOREWORD

Like about everybody else in the world, the first time I ever saw Seve Ballesteros was on television in 1976, when he damned near beat Johnny Miller in the British Open. I was here at home, taking it easy with a bad back, when I shouted to my wife, "Claudia, come in and watch, this kid has got to be something."

What I liked about him then, and still do, is that nothing scares him. Even if the rough's high and the wind's blowing good, he doesn't take a back seat. He doesn't have second place in mind, or third, or missing the cut. The only thing on his mind is winning and, honestly, I can't say the rest of us are that way. He's a lot like Arnold Palmer – he'll make a three on one hole and a ten on the next – and that's why he's getting all the galleries. He's exciting.

As I remember, the first time I met Seve, flesh-to-flesh, was at the Masters in 1977. We had a practice round together and I told him he could win the Masters if he came a week early to get used to the greens. And he did, of course, three years later. I've played with Seve a lot since then and I probably know him better than anybody else out on the tour. There are many similarities between us. We come from the same backgrounds, more or less, where growing up next to a golf course didn't mean a 10,000-square foot house and gold faucets in the bathrooms. We were both hungry and we're ready to go play where the money is – where the appearance money is, too.

Also, we've got the same temperament. When I first came out on the tour I said I would never play in the Masters again. I didn't like it, blah blah, and later I admitted that if there was anything I'd ever take back, that was it. Same with Seve. When he showed up late for the US Open at Baltusrol in 1980 and got disqualified he said he'd never play in the tournament again. That's the old Latin blood, and it's something that can't be held against him. Latins say things that fifteen seconds later they would give thousands of dollars to take back.

Over on this side of the water there are a lot of players who want me to say Seve's wild, or Seve's lucky, and I tell them that that's part of the game; they're just jealous because when you total up your score at the end of the day it's not how, it's how much.

You'll never hear the great players say he's lucky; they'll say he's great, though. How great? Every generation or so there emerges a golfer who is a little bit better than anyone else. I believe Ballesteros is one of them. It won't be long before he's the greatest international player of all time. I'd say even more successful than Gary Player who, right now, is the finest international player who ever held a golf club; and Roberto De Vicenzo was fantastic. But Seve, before he retires, should be better than them all.

On a golf course he's got everything – I mean *everything*: touch, power, know-how, courage and charisma. By the time he finishes, in about twenty years, he may not be equal to Jack Nicklaus – nobody will ever be equal to Jack Nicklaus – but he'll be more than equal to all the rest of us – myself, Watson, Byron Nelson and even Ben Hogan. Seve Ballesteros, through the 1980s, will be the successor to Jack Nicklaus.

Lee Trevino

Dallas, February, 1982.

6

CHAPTER ONE

THE VIEW FROM PEDRENA

"Oh, Severiano, you have left the English and Americans like destroyed eagles."

From a ballad sung in Pedreña

The old stone farmhouse, on a hill above the Bay of Santander, commands a westward view of the northern coastline of Spain. The hills, rolling on to the north, obscure the vast Bay of Biscay but, straight ahead, across the smaller bay, one can see the grey gables of the Palacio de la Magdalena, a Royal summer home. Inland, the long green shoulder of the Cantabrian mountains separates the maritime province of La Montana from the body of Spain.

In the middle distance are the stooping *pescadoras*, bare-footed women with their skirts hitched up, fanned out across the beach, digging for clams. Nearer still, just under the farmhouse, lie the green fairways and pine trees of Real Club de Golf de Pedreña, the finest course and the most exclusive golf club in northern Spain. At the time our story opens, in January 1977, the honorary presidents of the club are the late King Alfonso XIII, at whose request the club was built in 1929, and his son King Juan Carlos I, whose son, Juan Carlos of Bourbon, had two months earlier acceded to Head of State upon the death of General Franco.

The morning is cold, and as though to keep warm the *pescadoras* are chatting briskly among themselves and giggling. One of them, rising to stretch her back, calls flirtatiously down the beach to where a young golfer is posing for a London photographer. The golfer is Severiano Ballesteros, nick-

named 'Seve', pronounced 'Sebbie' in Spanish. He blushes at the girl, an old schoolmate, and resumes his photo session. He hits balls, mostly chips and punched irons, for about half an hour. It is an impressive performance, not only in its shot-making but in its sense of ritual. Deftly and indifferently, he drags each ball into place and settles in. He gathers his concentration, hits the ball, watches its flight, taps his club clean on the side of his toe and drags up another ball. A look of frustration begins to creep over his face until, at last yielding to temptation, he sets his feet firmly into the sand and lashes a ball up over the water. It climbs higher and higher, over some distant fishing boats and disappears into a far, wooded hill.

The soles of your feet tingle as you watch, and when Ballesteros turns to grin you suddenly share his feeling: the pure joy of hitting a ball. Here, at the age of 19, is the most exciting golfer to come out of Europe since Tony Jacklin. Indeed, in only a few years it will be commonly felt throughout the world that Ballesteros is the most exciting player to enter the game since Arnold Palmer burst on the scene in the late 1950s. The towering shot puts an end to the photo session. "Okay?" he says. The decision to stop, while ringing with authority, seems neither abrupt nor discourteous. Ballesteros is in command.

He starts to collect the loose balls, idly reaching down and turning the club face under each before, with a quick flick, nipping it straight up in the air. The ball bounces once on the face of the club then plops into the practice bag he holds open in his other hand. Seeing you enthralled, he says, "Watch." The

next ball is nipped high. It comes down – click! – off the face of the club and then, in diminishing bounces – click-click-clickclick-click – settles dead on the flat face of the iron. Ballesteros cradles the ball. He starts bouncing it again and, rather like a girl in a schoolyard, swings one leg and then the other between the clubhead and the bouncing ball. He is not showing off, for he too enjoys watching such legerdemain. He stops abruptly: next act. His arm dangles down and the ball settles dead on the upturned face of the club. "Like this we used to have races as little boys," he says, and starts running. The races were a form of egg and spoon, only with club and ball. Who won? Seve stops and shrugs.

Ballesteros presents a striking, monochromatic figure, white V-neck pullover worn over a dark roll-top sweater. Long, heavy hair, as black and layered as a raven's wing, is set against a ruddy complexion. He is a big man, 6ft. tall and 13 stone 10 pounds, handsome and, by turns, radiant and uncommonly

grim or, appropriately in Spanish, "severo". A brooding look, which can frighten even his friends, can cross his face as suddenly and fleetingly as a cloud shadow. "Let's go," he says now, and, following him, one notices the tilt of his shoulders, his right one dropping lower than his left. What is more, his right arm is longer than his left, with the overall result that the right hand hangs about two inches lower. As he walks, his left hand dangles curiously limp while his right swings through an arc.

Seve's brother, Manuel, awaits in a car on a quay. A broken road and then a dirt track lead up the hill above the village of Pedreña (pop.: 5,000), to the farmhouse built by their mother's grandparents in 1882. It is neat: green doors and shutters, a red tile roof. The house stands in the centre of a small plot of land, with an outside well to serve it: the illusion is cast of a small-holding, struggling family. Actually, the Ballesteroses, even before the youngest son achieved fame and fortune, had accumulated untold *carros de tierra* – packets of land. If not wealthy, the family is near to it.

"Come and see the cows first," Seve says, leading the way to the stables which are tucked under and form part of the farmhouse. There are three cows, a donkey and a wire pen filled with rabbits. Ballesteros identifies each animal by name. His eye catches a bird's nest in the rafters. A look of tenderness comes over his face. *"Las golondrinas,"* he says in Spanish. "The swallows, they have gone south for the winter."

Next to the stables is the basement of the house. It is dark, except for an orange glow from the wood-burning stove on the dirt floor in the corner. A heavy canvas cloth hangs from a low rafter; it is into this that Ballesteros drives golf balls in the evenings or when the winter days are cold and wet. The room looks too cramped for such exercise but Seve, to prove otherwise, draws a club from a nearby bag and swings it, full and clear of the rafters, smashing a ball into the canvas. The image is incongruous: a modern Japanese steel golf-club shaft flickering in the light of an old, Spanish cast-iron stove. *Crack-slap.* The family's German pointer snuffles in out of the cold to investigate the noise. He is called 'Blaster', after the name written on a sand wedge which an American tourist years ago gave Ballesteros.

A dark staircase, covered in threadbare linoleum, leads to the living quarters and, inevitably, the kitchen where Seve's mother is brewing coffee. The señora is a plump, comfortable little woman with a round face and a golden glint to her smile. She wears a woollen tea-cosy cap, tugged down with a sense of defiant humour. She knows no English, and makes no stab at it. Her feet are planted square, formidably. The families of the area are said to be even more matriarchal than elsewhere in Spain.

Across her sink, past the earthenware urn that holds drinking water, she has a fine view of Santander, the beach and a practice area of the Royal Pedreña course. Her brother, Ramon Sota, is down there giving a lesson. Even at this distance one can see a likeness to his sister: a short, chunky figure with a full face, but rather than a woollen cap he wears a checked one he bought years ago in London's Soho. In the late 1960s and early 70s Sota was the finest golfer in Spain. A player of no noticeable elegance, he won the Open championships of Spain, Portugal, France, Italy, Holland and Brazil and made six journeys to the US Masters tournament, coming joint sixth in 1965, the year Jack Nicklaus won his second title. It was at the time the finest finish a Spaniard ever achieved in a major American tournament.

Sota and his brother, Marceíno, forged the first link between the Ballesteros family's agrarian forebears and the world of professional golf. Like his nephews who followed him, he began as a Pedreña caddy and was not often allowed to play on the course.

Seve watches his uncle for a moment before resuming his guided tour. Across the hall is his own bedroom. For such a big man, Seve sleeps in a surprisingly narrow bed. The room, too, is small and has no windows. Three pictures hang on the wall. One is a colour reproduction of the Sacred Heart; the second is a primitive oil painting that depicts an uncle standing rigidly beside a cow; the third, from the same amateur brush as the primitive, is a retouched photograph of a solemn little boy dressed in his Sunday-best and holding an ice-cream cone. The boy, the family's first-born child, died at the age of two as a result of a wasp's stings. There were to be four more children, all boys, from the marriage of Baldomero Ballesteros Presmanes and Carmen Sota Ocejo.

The boys, all adults now and all professional golfers, are home together – a rare occasion. They are with their father in the small sitting room, made cozy and cramped by shelves full of trophies. Eldest of the boys is Baldomero Jr. – nicknamed 'Merin', pronounced 'Marine' – a club professional down the coast of Galacia at La Zapateira in La Coruna. Neat, handsome, round-faced and rubicund, Merin is 29, ten years older than

Seve, and is very much an elder-brother figure.

Then comes Manuel, a respected player on the European circuit who has often played in representative European sides against British and World teams. At 26, he is generously sacrificing his chances as a competitor by shepherding his young brother round the international circuit. 'Manolo' is, oddly, fair-haired, yet he has the fleetingly bleak look of a Ballesteros. Finally, Vicente, 24, slim and narrow-faced, holds a plum professional's club job at La Peñaza, near an American Air Base, over the mountains at Zaragoza.

The commanding male Ballesteros figure is their father, Baldomero Sr. At 58, he looks as fit now as he must have when he was a

powerful, youthful distance runner: tall and lean, with a craggy face and lithe, strong hands. An ugly scar rests on the heel of his left hand, a relic of the Spanish Civil War. The Ballesteroses were followers of Franco but at the outset of hostilities the province of Santander was Republican. On 20 June, 1937, Baldomero was recruited against his will into the Republican Army. Nine days later, in protest, he shot himself through the left hand. He was tried, convicted of the self-mutilation and sentenced to 20 years in prison. He was scarcely out of hospital, however, when Santander fell to Franco's troops in August of that year. Ballesteros fought with the Franquistas for the remainder of the war.

Ballesteros Sr. offers whiskey, wine and calvados all round while the Señora brings in a tray of coffee – for all bar Seve, who is given a glass of milk. The other Ballesteros men exchange glances, smile, and for a moment Seve looks embarrassed. Clearly the baby of

Victory: Baldomero sr., sixth from the left in the stern of the Pedreña *trainera*, the open fishing boat, after the village crew triumphed in the annual regatta in the Bay of Santander.

the family is *consentido*, spoilt. This fact, an uncontested family joke, leads on to a good-natured argument. Which of the men is the strongest, fastest, brightest, stingiest, hardest-working and best kicker of a football? Claims and counter-claims are advanced, with hot refutations, and agreement is reached in one category only: Seve is the best golfer. His mother nods her woolly-capped head, and rises to fetch her young son another glass of milk. "*Seve será el major golfista del mundo.*" The tone of her voice brooks no discussion. Seve will be the greatest golfer in the world.

Señora Ballesteros's defiant assumption, like her husband's gunshot wound, was the gesture of a *montañes*. The Ballesteroses and Sotas are *montañeses*. These are people of the Cantabrian mountains and seacoast round Santander, the industrial provincial capital that lies just west of the Basque country and some 100 miles round the corner from France. *Montañeses* are to Spain rather what Cornishmen are to England; in fact, these Spaniards share drops of Celtic blood with their northern brethren. They are brave, puzzling, resourceful, suspicious, superstitious and sometimes thrifty to the point of meanness. "They are lazy, too," Seve's mother will add, joking. "They sit around in taverns all day and play *tute*."

"The ancient land of Cantabria was immortalized in the heroic resistance of its inhabitants to Roman power," a Santander tourist brochure points out. "Later it was an important base for the Reconquest of the peninsula from the Moors. During the Middle Ages, the Brotherhood formed by the coastal towns became prosperous with their ships which were used for most of the commerce by sea to the north." And to the west, too, for among those who sailed out to discover the Americas were men from the Cantabrian coast: navigators, cartographers and, later, trader merchants who carried out wool, flour and eucalyptus wood in return for the riches of the New World.

It is to these men and the coastline that a monument, *El Monumento al Indiano y a la Marina de Castilla*, is erected in the nearby mountains. In Spanish 'Indiano' means "a

Seve, aged 8, holds a book, but his eyes seem on some distant green.

Spaniard returning rich from America."

Legend accompanies such seafaring folk. In Pedreña, the hilly village across the bay from Santander, a story survives that might have come from the pages of Daphne du Maurier. It maintains that bonfires were lit on the nearby sea cliffs when storms raged at sea. Passing ships, lured on to the rocks, were dashed to pieces; their sailors were drowned, their cargoes of silver and copper picked clean. The people of Pedreña today, according to a local newspaper, *Alerta*, are "fishermen, oarsmen and farm workers – often all at the same time." Of these, the *remeros*, the oarsmen, are the most famous throughout Spain. They row in the *Regata de Traineras*, an annual three-mile race round Santander Bay. The *trainera* is an open rowing boat, rather like a lifeboat, some forty feet long and peculiar to the north of Spain. The regattas are said to date back to the early 18th century and have continued nearly unbroken since 1861, when one was staged for the visiting Queen Isabel II.

In the elder Baldomero's lifetime the interest in the regattas has redoubled and the contests are now a highlight of the summer sporting season on the bay. Baldomero was an oarsman. On five different occasions he rowed in the Pedreña boat to national championships and, in 1946, he and his thirteen fellow *remeros* set a record in the race that still stands.

Baldomero Senior's grandfather, Manuel – Seve's great-grandfather – was known in church circles. He was an eminent bell-founder, and his bells still peel out from – among other places – the cathedrals at Toledo and Burgos. His son, Seve's grandfather, helped him at the foundry and in the campaniles, and, upon the old man's death, turned his hand to the family's dairy cattle farm. His son, Seve's father, started on the farm. After the Civil War he married Seve's mother whose family had for generations farmed the valley of the River Cubas in Pedreña. It was Seve's maternal grandfather who, in 1928, sold what was to become parts of the first, fourth and sixth holes of the Real Club de Golf de Pedreña. Severiano Ballesteros Sota was born in the farmhouse on 9 April, 1957. At the age of 7, he was given his first club or, more exactly, his first *part* of a club: a rusty old head of a 3-iron. Seve cleaned it and shined it and, wandering off into the fields, gathered up sticks for its shafts. He would hide these sticks from his brothers and,

The Once and Future Champion: Seve in action at the age of 10. John Jacobs, the eminent golf teacher, saw young Ballesteros play four years after these pictures were taken. "I said then that he had more ability than anyone I had ever seen in my life," Jacobs recalls, "not only because he obviously had talent and power but because he had balance and clubface control. These in a technical sense are demonstrated in these pictures. Right from an early age, Seve was using his clubface to its maximum and hitting the ball a very long way. Also, he's using what looks like a 5-iron; which is nice because this reminds us of the virtues of learning the game with one club."

Jacobs speaks of the first photo: "The body turn and shoulder position are just about perfect but the takeaway is too flat. Look at his hands. He has worked the clubhead behind him, rather than up, with his hands and arms, but this is understandable with a kid who wants to give the ball a very big hit. Only when he gets stronger will he be able to get power from a more upright, controlled takeaway. This picture interests me because somebody, probably one of his older brothers, could see the takeaway was too flat and got him to swing more upright. In doing so he got his shoulders one under the other too much and when he burst on the scene in 1976 he was *too* upright. It's interesting that at 12 his body and shoulder turns were better than they were at 19, at Royal Birkdale, when he was pushing and hooking a lot."

The second photo. "Look what a marvellous position Seve's in in his follow-through. The body is right out and away, which comes from a full shoulder turn. That clubhead is really whistling, carrying him right through. We don't know where the ball is going, true, because we don't know if the clubface was open or closed. But Seve's certainly given it a tremendous cuff – and that's the point: he's uninhibited, and that's wonderful in a little boy."

as needed, fetch one out, cut it to length, whittle a point in the slender end and drive it into the hosel, the round socket at the top of the iron head. He would then soak the assembly overnight in a bucket of water to allow the shaft to swell up snugly into the hosel. It was an ingenuous club, but a crude one: a heavy iron head on a frail and whippy shaft; it broke almost daily, and there was no grip.

The balls Seve chose to use were cruder still: stones.

"We wouldn't give him our balls, they were too precious," Baldomero Jr. recalls with a grin. "Seve would hunt along the beach for stones the size of golf balls, and fill his pockets with them. He would hide these stones, just as he did his shrub sticks, and make a little course by digging holes in the dirt on the farm. He also made courses on the beach. It is true – he would drive, chip and putt with these stones. In this way my brother learned to play golf."

By 8, Seve had begun to caddy – at 25 pence a day – and owned his first proper club. It was a genuine 3-iron given him by Manuel. "It was part of him," his brother recalls. "Without it he could not exist – he was like a man with no legs." With it Seve could smash a ball from their farmhouse over a stand of pine trees and on to the second green – a shot of some 150 yards.

Except on rare occasions, caddies were not allowed on the course – Uncle Ramon, the pro, saw to that – and Seve could not pursue these glorious shots. Instead he would steal on to the forbidden ground in the late evening, on moonlit nights and at dawn. "Sometimes it was difficult to see," he recalls, "and when you hit a ball you had to turn your ear and listen. If there was no sound, that was good – you were on the fairway. If there was a noise that was bad – you were in the trees."

Ballesteros's favourite world, illicitly lived in and therefore more real, was Pedreña's second hole. He played it a thousand times. A hearty par 3, it stretches 198 yards and is named 'La Rivera' after the River Cubas that runs through Pedreña. Over the passing years he was to measure his growing strength against the hole. "My brothers,

much bigger than me, used irons to reach the greens," he recalls, "but I had to borrow a wood. I was furious. My ambition was to be able to use an iron. I would ask, 'When will I be big enough?' And my brothers would answer 'Soon, soon.'"

Ballesteros was a boxing fan. It was while boxing as a child that he suffered what might have been the initial back injury that was to plague him in later life. He tripped and fell backwards on to the end of his spine and for a fortnight moved awkwardly and in pain. He was also a keen cyclist, swimmer and footballer. He played little tennis but years later he felt, with practice, he might have risen near to the top of that sport. His first sports cup, a giant thimble, Ballesteros won in a gruelling 1,500-metre foot race. "My friend, Javier, couldn't keep up with me even on a bicycle," he says proudly. "I won the race by sixteen seconds."

Even then, he was a gambler. "I always bet more than I can afford to lose," he recalls. "That made me try harder – and I never lost." Like most fierce competitors, Seve remembers statistics. At the age of 9, he sneaked round the Pedreña course with two clubs in an hour. At 10, he played in his first caddy competition. He scored a 10 on the first hole and finished fifth in 51 strokes, and in a flood of tears. At 11, he came second in 42 strokes. At 12, playing over a full round, he won the competition with a 79, nine strokes over par on the 6,315-yard course of narrow hilly fairways. Still 12, he was playing to the equivalent of a scratch handicap; Ballesteros may well have been the most precocious player in the history of golf, more advanced for his age than even the great Bobby Jones.

That summer, 1969, was a watershed for Seve. He carried Manuel's bag in the Santander Open at Pedreña. During a practice round Manuel played with the established Spaniards Jose Cabo and Manuel Calero. "In those days, Seve was learning by imitation," recalls Manuel, who went on to win the tournament. "When we asked him to play a few holes with us he tried to chip like me, putt like Calero and drive like Cabo. And still he scored par after par."

Father and son: the Ballesteroses watch the 1979 *trainera* race from a power boat.

Seve also got his first golf shoes that summer, an oversized pair discarded by a club member. "I remember waiting to grow up enough to wear Manuel's shoes," Seve recalls, adding with unconscious irony, "but by the time I could wear my brother's shoes I had my own." By the age of 13 he had beaten his brother for the first time. "The next year he beat me quite a lot," Manuel says. "It made me very happy."

Seve was not so generous. He not only expected the best from himself but the same from others – a severity that was to break down more than one caddy in the future – and when Manuel played badly in the 1970 Spanish Under 25s championship, 13-year-old Seve roared at him for playing so stupidly. He flung down his brother's bag, saying that he could have played better himself, and threatened to resign as his caddy.

If Seve learned by imitating his brother's peers he also owes a greater debt than he might acknowledge to his uncle. For all his clumsy moves, Ramon's techniques can still be seen in Ballesteros's game: the solid, patient set-up, the care and scrutiny in the take-away, the sudden pauses to check the set of the hands, the deep thought. "Ramon wouldn't help Seve much in his game, that's true," says Manuel Piñero, perhaps the most perceptive of all Spanish players. "But he showed him that somebody from Pedreña could go out into the world, and win."

The world beckoned. Ballesteros was impatient to get out into it. The National Primary School in Pedreña left him cold. He played truant frequently, ignoring the masters and, early on, his mother, who told him there was

Seve, with his mother, Carmen, who from the start said her son would be a world-beater. The old Ballesteros home is in the background.

no future in golf. He would gaze out of the window and dream of winning championships: "Every one in the world, and by twenty strokes."

The fiery youngster knew what he wanted. At 14, he gave up alcohol. "I used to have white wine at lunch. It never affected me," he says. "I smoked a little too, but I saw that all the good players didn't drink or smoke. So I said to myself, 'Seve, if you want to be a great player you stop.' So I stop."

By then it was only a matter of time before Ballesteros turned professional. In the summer of 1973, aged 16, he effectively lost his amateur status by accepting a full set of promotional golf clubs and a bag from an American army officer who was stationed near brother Vicente's club in Zaragoza. The brand-name, 'SUPER', was emblazoned on the bag and, responding to such flattery, Seve not only looked like a pro but played like one. In his farewell caddy championship he returned a 65, to win in a walk.

On the first day of the following January, having fulfilled all the required conditions, Severiano Ballesteros Sota was duly awarded his 'player's card' by the Royal Spanish Golf Federation, the ruling body that also controls the Spanish Professional Golfers' Association. He had returned satisfactory Standard Scratch Score cards, passed a written test on the Rules of Golf and paid 5,000 pesetas membership fee to become – at 16 years 8 months and 21 days – the youngest accredited professional tournament player in the history of Spanish golf.

Games for the Young and not so Young

When I was a boy in Pedrena, dreaming about winning every tournament in the world, it was necessary for my friends and I to practise the game in many strange ways. For example, we had to learn to make all our golf shots with one club because we only had one club; or we played golf at night, when we could sneak on the course, or on the beach or with a caddy bag over our shoulder. At the time we didn't think these things were good or bad for our game. But, looking back, it certainly helped me to learn golf. If you are young – or not so young – try these children's games: they will help you understand the game better and, also, they are fun.

One-club golf: When you are young and have every club in the bag, let me tell you, it makes the game of golf look too easy. You don't concentrate. You don't *think*. You don't take time to study the rough or the bunkers or the bumps in the fairway. If you have only one club, maybe a 3-iron as I did or a 5-iron like Lee Trevino used as a boy, you must always think hard about the rough and the sand and the lie of the land. Let me give you an example; here is how I played a 3-iron out of a green-side bunker:

Open the face wide, until the loft becomes about the same as a sand wedge, then set up and aim about *fifty yards* to the left of the flag. Then, swinging outside and in, play the shot as full as you would an orthodox sand wedge shot, breaking the right wrist as you make contact with the sand behind the ball. This will help put 'stop' on the ball and, as you practise the shot, you will feel a "touch" coming into your bunker play. Your judgement of sand and distance will improve, too, and later your bunker play with a sand wedge will be more confident.

The one club, you will soon see, teaches you to invent shots and work with your hands. For another example, putt with a 3-iron, pushing your hands far forward, until your club face becomes the loft of a putter. It helps you to use your hands on other shots and, of course, improves that 'feel' for the ball. Also, it keeps you thinking. Children – *everybody* – get lazy and sometimes stop thinking on a golf course.

Night-putting: Practising your putting when it is almost dark helps your golf putting habits and gives you confidence. It does all this for one reason – you can't see anything (except maybe a dim hole in the distance) and this takes away the temptation to watch where the ball is going after you hit it. Instead, you can keep your head down and watch only the line of your stroke – which is the way you should putt.

Bag-and-Umbrella Putting: This little "game" got started when we were caddying as boys. When club members were going from one green to the next tee, we would drop a ball quickly and putt three or four times with their putter before running to see where their balls went off the next tee. It turned out that this was good practice because you would have to stand very still over the ball or the golf bag would slide off your shoulder. The same thing with a member's umbrella: if you had to hold an umbrella under your chin when you putted, you had to hold your head still, or the umbrella would fall.

So, I have told you three 'games' that helped me form good habits as a young golfer. There are other things I must tell you if you are young and starting the game. First, hit the ball *hard*. Don't worry too much where it goes, but hit it hard. This makes you aggressive and when you are young you *must* be aggressive, or you will never grow up to be a winner. Third, *compete*! I used to bet for more money than I had in my pocket. That made me try

very, very hard because I had no choice, I *had* to win. I never lost – that's true!

Finally, and this is for parents: you must always tell your child that he or she is good, the best. My brothers and my mother and father always told me I would become the best golfer in the world and, let me tell you, it was good for my confidence. You must always build up a child's confidence. It is the beginning of a good golf game.

First Tips: play with one club and even a bag or umbrella

CHAPTER TWO

ON THE ROAD

"He's a gorilla off the tee. He's out of control, certainly, but that goes with being young."

Billy Casper, on first playing with Ballesteros in 1975

He came down the hill, a bag of clubs over his shoulder, and took the bus from Pedreña to Santander, where he caught the overnight train through the mountains to Madrid. From there, Ballesteros left Spain for the first time in his life, travelling – also for the first time – in an airplane, on his way to his first international golf tournament: the 1974 Portuguese Open.

The flight to Lisbon was tough. Ballesteros recalls enjoying the lift and plunge of the plane – it felt like a Ferris wheel ride. Also, he recalls more pensive moments during the flight when he wondered if he had chosen the right career. "I remember telling myself, over and over, 'Seve, there is no turning back. Golf is the only direction you can go. Golf is the only thing you can do.'"

And, of late, he wasn't doing it well. A fortnight earlier Seve had competed in his first professional tournament, the Spanish PGA championship, which brought a field of 110 players to the old and honoured Club de Golf de San Cugat, Barcelona. Seve started the week promisingly. On the first day, in practice, he scored 27 over the outward nine holes, an astonishing performance. As the championship began he was bubbling with confidence. The bubbles soon broke. He finished twentieth in the championship, and felt humiliated. Manuel Piñero, another competitor, remembers finding Ballesteros alone in the locker room after the last round. "He was sobbing, his head on his knees," Piñero says. "He actually expected to win. He *always* expects to win." Seve's prize money that week was £15.

Even so, money was no pressing prob-

lem. He had been loaned $1,000 by a patron, Dr. Cesar Campuzano, a native of Santander and prosperous Madrid radiologist who spent summer golfing holidays in Pedreña. The loan, which Seve later paid back, was to cover his expenses to play over the following month in the Portuguese, Spanish, Madrid and French Open championships, the first Continental phase of the annual European circuit run by the British PGA.

The doctor had seen Seve play, but being no expert his faith was largely based on word of mouth. All of Spanish golf knew of the shy, raw *montañes*, Manuel's magical little brother. Older Spanish players, speaking the summer before to British golf writers, had shaken their fingers in awe of the boy. "One day he will be better than all of us," they had said. "You watch. You will see."

We, the British Press, might have come across Seve in that 1974 Portuguese Open, but none of us remembers him. The championship was being played early in April, at the holiday course of Estoril, a tram ride from Lisbon. Overlooking the grey Atlantic, Estoril is a charming course, with a par of only 69. At 5,656 yards, it is probably among the shortest championship courses in the world; yet it is by no means easy, for its narrow fairways wander through pines, mimosa shrubs and thickets of eucalyptus: one wild shot and a player is imprisoned by tree trunks. Ballesteros served such sentences in his qualifying round. "I was all over the place that day, in the trees, out of bounds, in the bunkers, in the water, everywhere but on the green," he recalls. "My trouble was that off every tee I tried to put the ball in the hole."

His score was a disaster: 43 strokes over the outward nine holes; 46 coming home. His 89, exactly 20 strokes over par, was the worst

The Santander Bay Area. A popular Spanish summer resort, for both the public and the monarchy, the north coast of the peninsula is blessed with the Real Club de Golf de Pedreña. Its roots are both royal and British. The club was built in 1929 at the request of King Alfonso XIII. Alfonso's son, Juan de Bourbon, who never ascended to the throne because of Franco's dictatorship, played golf at Pedreña and, on exile at Estoril, reached a four handicap level, several times representing Spain in her national amateur teams. His son, the present King Juan Carlos, was a keen but mediocre player until his security advisors suggested he give up the game because of the risks of assassination. Pedreña was designed by the British firm of Colt, Allison and Morrison with Scottish links in mind; now watered by sprinklers, the nearest the hilly course comes to a Scottish links is the sheep that graze on the roughs during the winter.

---

among those attempting to qualify. What was more, he had scored it on 9 April, his 17th birthday! Seve again dissolved into tears. "I remember thinking, 'Seve, Dr. Campuzano put his confidence in you. Manuel put his confidence in you. And you let them down.' But the Doctor was there, and he said to me, 'Don't worry, you are the best.'"

Ballesteros was in the air by the time the championship proper had begun and at La Manga, practising for the Spanish Open, by the time it was won by the Welshman, Brian Huggett. At La Manga there was to be great

excitement when two heroes of the US Masters, just completed at Augusta, flew in. Seve's idol, Gary Player, had won, while Maurice Bembridge had tied the course record with a final round of 64; any news of Ballesteros's fine qualifying score of 71 was buried in the fuss over their arrival. That evening, after watching Player hit practice balls in the sunset, Seve dined with some fellow Spaniards. "We talked about the highest scores each of us ever scored on a hole and when somebody said he once scored a ten at Royal Birkdale, I said, 'Impossible! Nobody can score double figures on one hole!'" With that remark Ballesteros tempted the gods . . .

The next morning Seve was paired with the sad-faced French Basque, Jean Garaialde, a veteran who five years earlier had won the championship. Seve opened with eight straight pars, bringing him to one of the most dramatic holes in Europe, which was being played that week as the ninth. The hole lies in the shadow of a mountain range, with the Mediterranean sparkling off to the east; it plunges down 586 yards between rocky ravines that are spotted with scrub and ice-blue cacti. The fairway then swings left past an artificial lake before climbing to expire on an enormous, rolling green. Out of bounds lie left and right of the tee.

The temptation to smash a 300-yard drive was too much for the young Spaniard. He hooked his first ball out of bounds. He sliced his second ball out of bounds. He reloaded and smashed his third – his fifth shot on the card – straight down the fairway. As they walked off the tee, the Frenchman tried to calm the youngster. *"Estate tranquilo,"* he said. Keep calm. Don't worry. *"Mala suerte."* Bad luck. Ballesteros glowered at the Frenchman, swore and beat his driver into the ground. "I was very much furious," he recalls. "And I think maybe Garaialde was afraid what I might do."

Ballesteros splashed his sixth shot into the lake. He dropped out under penalty, chipped into the bunker and finally got down in eleven strokes. "I walked off the green looking to see if my friends were watching and thinking of what I had said the night before. *Estupido!*" Ballesteros scored 83 that day and 78 the next, missing the cut by one shot.

He was not so stupid to pass up the opportunity of studying the great players practising. He looked with particular interest at the grooved, effortless swing of the eventual winner, the American Jerry Heard, a man as big as himself. "Watching him I could see my swing was much too fast, and that night I tried to imitate his slow rhythm. I also tried to copy his take-away – very slow, very good." He also watched Player practising in the bunkers. "'*Manos de Plata,*' we call him in Spanish, 'hands of silver.' What I learned was the way he gets a solid stance in the bunker and then locks his legs forward."

Ballesteros came away from that championship, his first in a top-class international field, with mixed feelings: there was much to learn but, even so, he secretly felt himself already the best player in the world. "My trouble in those days was I always studied the players," he recalled years later. Then – remembering the temptation that had destroyed him on the ninth tee that day at La Manga – "but I never studied the courses."

Ballesteros's scores didn't improve much over the next fortnight. At the Madrid Open at Pueta de Hierro in Madrid he played poorly, shot 84–79 and missed the cut: he was gone by the time little Piñero, only 21, won the title. At the French Open at Chantilly Seve again missed the cut, this time again by a single stroke. He stayed to watch the eventual winner, Peter Oosterhuis. The young Spaniard was, and still is hugely impressed by the big Englishman's solid putting stance and his touch in stroking long putts.

Manuel advised Seve to abandon the tour as it went on to Britain the following week, and to return to Pedrena. Seve took the advice, and as he returned home he felt that deep sense of desolation he had felt in Portugal: he had let down his brother and his sponsor.

Back at Pedreña, he practised long hours and, in need of money, suffered the indignity of caddying again, for 25p a round, while in distant Sussex his new touring colleagues were battling through the Penfold tournament. He felt moments of panic, too, as his childhood friends spoke of their secure, if modest careers: cement factory worker, bank teller, cargo clerk at the Santander airport. And, once again, Ballesteros told himself: there was no turning back.

Within a month, however, he had won his first professional tournament: the National Under-25s championship for Professionals which was played over his home course at Pedreña. He won it by restraining the wild, flailing swing which had been crippling his game. It would be encouraging to suggest that this restraint was the result of growing wisdom on Ballesteros's part. "I had no choice," he admits. "I had to swing slow that week. The glue in the hosels of my clubs was drying up and cracking, and if I swung hard the clubheads would fly off." Even so, the victory was especially satisfying, for not only was it his first as a professional but it carried with it a winner's purse of $1,000. The following week Ballesteros came second in the Santander Open and the week after that he won the Vizcaya tournament in Bilbao,

O*le!* An early, characteristic image of the Spaniard (then 19), as a putt drops.

with brothers Manuel second and Vicente third. These may have been regional tournaments but, no matter, the doctor's faith had been vindicated.

In October, bursting with renewed confidence, Seve set out again on the international trail, playing in the Italian Open at the Lido in Venice. The competition was strong, led by the top American money-winner of the year, Johnny Miller, and the man who still dominated Europe, Oosterhuis. The first round was reduced to nine holes because of fog rising from the lagoons. On the putting green afterwards players came up to Manuel Ballesteros to congratulate him on his 33, which shared the lead at the end of the day. "That wasn't me," said Manuel, with more pride than resentment, "that was my little brother." Seve failed to keep up the pace that week but still finished fifth overall, five strokes behind the winner, Oosterhuis, and three adrift of Miller. His performance, as top Spaniard, earned him a place three weeks later in the Ibergolf Trophy.

Ibergolf, a course construction group, had invited nine players to this 36-hole competition at their new layout, Las Lomas el Bosque, a watery and wooded course near Madrid. Ballesteros returned the worst score of the competition, a 79, on the opening day and, mercurial man that he is, the best, a 69, on the next. He came fifth; the winner was Gary Player. The tournament finished on 10 November, a Sunday, and that evening Player and the Ballesteros brothers, Manuel and Severiano, flew to Lisbon to catch a flight to Johannesburg, where on Wednesday the South African PGA championship was to begin. "This time," recalls Seve, "I forgot my visa."

The brothers missed their flight and finally arrived in Johannesburg only a few hours before the first round of the championship. Ballesteros pieced together a groggy opening round of 74 while Player, who flies first-class and often catnaps in the aisle, was fresh enough to stay in touch with 70. Ballesteros had somewhat settled down by the end of the tournament and finished joint-26th, eighteen strokes behind Dale Hayes, who edged out

Ed Barner, who was advised to do business with the young Spaniard, with his breakthrough client, Johnny Miller.

Player to win by a single stroke. The brothers stayed on in South Africa for three more tournaments but, despite an eighth place tie in the Western Province Open, Seve made little impression.

Conversely, golf in South Africa made a strong impression on him. He was surprised at how little the black caddies were paid and years later regretted yielding to local pressure to pay them the low, customary wage. Worse, he was struck by the low level of their living standard. He recalls: "I will never forget the sight of black caddies grinding out cigarettes with their bare feet."

Ballesteros had completed his first year as a tournament professional. On the domestic table, his 1974 record was gratifying: 9th in the Spanish Order of Merit, with two victories, two seconds and a seventh place finish in eight tournaments. He had come 13th in the Continental Order of Merit. In the European table – that is, the British Order of Merit – his results were less impressive: 113th, which perhaps wasn't as bad as it looks for he had played in only five tournaments and thirteen rounds that counted. But his stroke average, 74.76, was a fair reflection on his reckless, attacking game and, as he himself confessed, his reluctance to study the subtleties of a golf course. Still, in 1974 he paid his way, a rare achievement among such fledglings. His earnings reached nearly £5,000.

In 1975, Ballesteros was to spread his wings, travelling to America, Japan and even Thailand. Most important, since he was to make them his second home, he made his maiden voyage to the British Isles where he underwent a painful initiation to the vagaries of seaside golf. The occasion was the Penfold PGA championship at Royal St. George's on the Kent coast at Sandwich. St. George's is

something special, a links that after being passed over for thirty-two years was to return to the Open rota in 1981. There are many who love those links as deeply as did the greatest of all golf writers, Bernard Darwin, who in 1919 evoked its spell in his famed book, *The Golf Courses of the British Isles*:

> A fine spring day, with the larks singing as they seem to sing nowhere else; the sun shining on the waters of Pegwell Bay and lighting up the white cliffs in the distance; this is as nearly my idea of Heaven as is to be attained on any earthly links.

By contrast, to Ballesteros Sandwich was

An early promotional sheet, sent out by the thousand from the UMI office in Los Angeles.

U·M·I SEVE BALLESTEROS

10880 WILSHIRE BOULEVARD ■ SUITE 1800 ■ LOS ANGELES, CALIFORNIA 90024 ■ PHONE (213)

CABLE: UMINTER ■ TELEX: 69-8166

his idea of Hell. "It was the first time I had ever seen an English course, and it was horrible," Ballesteros recalls. "So cold, so much wind, so much different from any other course I had known. Especially I didn't like the fact there were no trees for my eyes to get reference. I stayed in a private house. The only thing I can remember is that the man of the house would play the piano at two o'clock in the morning. I thought he was a little bit crazy. I tell you, by the time I had played one round I didn't like *anything* about Sandwich."

By the time he had completed a second round, adding an 84 to his opening 78, Ballesteros had missed the cut. First impressions are deep-set in golf – Bobby Jones, for example, lost his temper, picked up his ball, tore up his scorecard and walked away with a "puzzling dislike" of St. Andrews when he first played there in the 1921 championship – and after years of playing and failing there Ballesteros has yet to grow to like Sandwich.

In the more compatible climate of Spain, playing on the less challenging domestic tour, Ballesteros was taking control. He not only successfully defended his Under-25 title; he twice finished second and twice third in other Spanish tournaments, to lay a cornerstone for capturing the Order of Merit titles both in Spain and on representative international sides later in the year.

On his second visit to Britain, for the Open at Carnoustie, Ballesteros's game didn't match the bright and glorious weather. He had injured his foot while practising the previous week on the beach at Pedreña and, balance and rhythm gone, returned cards of 79 and 80 to miss the midway cut. By his third visit, in September, for the Double Diamond Championship at Turnberry, the course of Ballesteros's life was changed. He was in the Rest of the World side, which also included the South Africans Player and Hayes, the Australian Jack Newton and the New Zealander Bob Charles. The Americas team, which embraced Argentina, included the popular Roberto de Vicenzo, towards whom Spanish golfers are reverential.

Of de Vicenzo, then 52, there was much to be reverential about; prior to Ballesteros (and the great Mexican–American, Lee Trevino) he was the finest Spanish-speaking golfer of all time, with an enviable record of 165 world-wide tournament victories, including the 1967 Open.

At Turnberry, de Vicenzo was much impressed by the young Spaniard. One evening he called the American golfers' agent, Ed Barner, to his hotel room.

De Vicenzo, by tipping Seve, sought to repay the American for helping him solve a small problem he had recently faced over an air ticket.

The Argentinian turned an unsettling look on Barner and bade him sit down. "I am going to tell you something important," said de Vicenzo. "That Spanish boy, Ballesteros, can hit the ball. He has greatness within him." He did not expand on this oracular judgement, and Barner was left to make what he could of the words.

Barner, unlike his foremost rival manager, Mark McCormack, barely knew a birdie from a bunker. He had made his name as a show business promoter – the pop singer, Trini Lopez, was one client – but over the years he had taken on Johnny Miller, the hottest property in golf at the time, and Billy Casper, both Mormons like himself, as well as the evergreen Sam Snead and the less luminous 1969 US Open champion Orville Moody. Barner wanted to expand his business.

Now he went straight to Casper, who was playing that week with the Americans. Casper agreed to play a practice round with Seve the following fortnight at the Lancome Trophy competition near Paris. The American, like de Vicenzo, is not given to exaggeration; but his judgement was handed down to Barner like a tablet from on high. "Seve was not only a gorilla off the tee," said Casper.

¿**Q**ue dice, amigo? Ballesteros and the American, Lanny Wadkins. It was Wadkins who offered Seve the advice, correct but unheeded, that the boyhood clubs the Spaniard first brought on to the Tour were too whippy in the shafts, which partly accounted for his wild driving.

"He has undoubtedly the finest short game I had ever witnessed in my life."

In a field of some fair long hitters – Palmer, Jacklin, the Australian Bob Shearer, the American Lanny Wadkins as well as Casper, Player and Garaialde – Ballesteros put all to shame in the long-driving contest that preceded the event: he smashed a ball 293 yards. In the tournament itself Seve showed flashes of magic to come third, eight strokes behind Player. During one round Wadkins approached Seve with a tip. "You're making good passes at the ball but your clubs aren't fitting you," Wadkins said. "You're out of control because the shafts of your clubs are too whippy." Seve nodded. He didn't totally understand the American's Southern English – pure English was difficult enough – and, besides, he felt affection for his 'Super' clubs.

Barner, meanwhile, moved in. In the mellow stone clubhouse at Saint-Nom-la-Breteche, once a farmhouse for the court of Louis XIV, he dined during the tournament with Seve and Manuel. A briefcase rested by his chair. As Barner and Manuel talked, Seve ran his fingers up and down his orange-juice glass, not understanding a word until Manuel translated into Spanish. "If I can arrange for you both to come over and play in the Walt Disney World National Team championship in Florida in two weeks," Barner offered, Manuel translating, "would you stay over and try for your player's card for the American tour?"

Barner went further. He would arrange and pay for their travel from Como, where each was to play the following week in the Italian Open, to Miami and on to Disney World. He would pay their hotel bills. He would pay their living expenses while in Florida. He would pay their return flight fares to Spain. "If you win anything in the Disney Team championship pay me back what I lay out. Keep the difference," he concluded. "We'll talk about me representing you when we get there."

The hard sell set the Ballesteros boys back on their heels. They were flattered that Miller's, Heard's and Casper's agent was paying homage to Seve; although it was unclear at the time that Manuel would not be entered in the Qualifying School, unclear also to the innocent Spaniards that this was not a patron willing to give away money, but a businessman. Manuel's role would be travelling companion and translator for his younger brother. Still, there was nothing to lose. They agreed: they would go to America.

Their decision raised problems for Barner. At this late date there was no certainty he could get the unrenowned Ballesteros brothers entered in the Disney event, a four-round competition made up of two-men teams. "I was taking a step in the dark," Barner recalls. "But I knew I held the trump card." The trump card was more a bargaining chit: Johnny Miller, whom the Disney people desperately wanted, and who had first turned them down, was now keen to play. Also, Barner knew the organisers wanted an international flavour to their tournament; such spice would be added by the Spaniards.

Barner returned to his offices on Wilshire Boulevard in Los Angeles where he drew up a contract for Seve – but not one for Manuel – and got the brothers entered in the team championship which was to be held from 23 to 26 October. The Ballesteros brothers went to Lake Como where in hammering rain off the Alps the image of Barner was enhanced when Casper won. Seve, never in the hunt, tied for 12th place, his brother for 31st. Then they set out for America.

Barner flew to Miami, checked into a hotel and waited for them. The Spaniards duly arrived and, awestruck, made a leisurely trip to the course, only to realise they had missed their team starting time by four hours. Only through the advocacy of the American, Jim Colbert, were they allowed to play.

That evening they sought out Orville Moody. Moody, a part-Cherokee Indian from Oklahoma, could speak some Spanish and was companionable, but as a player he had achieved nothing since winning the US Open in 1969. Barner, he said (quite rightly) had not been able to earn him much money either through contracts or appearances. They sat long over a Spanish dinner. The Ballesteroses grew wary of Barner.

"I waited for five hours in my hotel room for them to show up," Barner recalls, "and I was getting *hot*. When they came they were nervous and sceptical. I told them that Moody might be a nice guy but he hadn't won *anything* since 1969 and that maybe we had better get things straight: I told them, 'Listen, I can only do you well if *you* do well. I can't sell a loser.' I told them the agreement I had in mind was for five years. I told them that at this moment no one even knew of Severiano Ballesteros. We talked back and forth and they said they wanted their Spanish attorney to look over the contract and I said, 'I *insist* your Spanish attorney looks it over.' So we wrote at the bottom of the contract 'subject to the approval of Severiano Ballesteros's attorney in Spain'. Manuel was a little upset that I wasn't interested in him, but I wasn't." Seve signed the contract which indeed was later to be approved in Spain.

In the Disney team tournament, won by the Americans Jim Colbert and Dean Refram, the Ballesteroses failed to make the two-round cut. Not a whit abashed, the next week Seve entered – to use its proper title – the Tournament Players Division of the Professional Golfers' Association of America's Fall Qualifying School for Approved Tournament Players. As a school it teaches the Rules of Golf, club repair, pro shop management and how to deal with the press. Most crucially, it was a 108-hole event to determine those worthy of joining the American tour.

The qualifying tournament is always brutal. That autumn 380 players were fighting for twenty-five tour places. The field was one of the most formidable in years. It included Jerry Pate, the American amateur wizard who the following summer was to win the US Open championship, and George Burns, Gary Koch and Bob Gilder, all of whom were later to make their mark. From the European tour, apart from Ballesteros, came the South African Dale Hayes, then aged 23, and already a proven winner.

Ballesteros began indifferently with a 77 and 75. Improving, he crept to the border of winning his card by the time he teed up on the sixth day. His playing partner was 'Corker' de Loach, a Tennessean and a popular, perennial Qualifying School failure. De Loach years later was to recall that last round. "Over those first nine holes, Ballesteros was the greatest player I had ever seen, anywhere. Putting, chipping. And *driving*, my God, he hit the ball long and straight and with terrific carry."

Opening on the more demanding homeward half of the course, Ballesteros scored a 33, three strokes under par. But as he later recalled, he became preoccupied during the last nine holes with thoughts of travelling the American circuit alone, without command of the language and half a world away from his family and Pedreña. "It was funny, but he kind of came apart on the last nine," De Loach recalls. "Once he got stuck under the lip of a trap and took a triple-bogie, then later, when I missed an itsy-bitsy putt on the same green, he came across and said, 'bad luck.' I remember thinking; 'you're telling *me* bad luck when you've just played yourself out a player's card!' It was a generous thing to say, but then Seve is a generous guy."

Ballesteros went on that day to score a homeward 40 for a round of 73. His six-round total, 441, fell four strokes above the mark for a card and eighteen behind the winner, Pate. At 18, hampered by pangs of loneliness and doubt, Ballesteros had narrowly missed be-

OK, where's the ball? The Spaniard, early and late in his career, was often found in the rough, as he was here at Wentworth in 1977.

coming the youngest player ever to earn his US tour card (the South African Bobby Cole was 19 when he won his in 1967). According to US PGA records, Seve would have been the youngest golfer ever to join the US tour.

Homesick or not, Ballesteros had further indoctrination in America. He travelled from Miami to Los Angeles to spend a fortnight with Ed Barner. "It was a tough time for Seve," his agent admits. "I think he is still uncomfortable, remembering those days at our house, alone and without his family."

Ballesteros's stay in California conformed much to a pattern. It began with 2½ hours of English lessons at Barner's downtown office, followed by games of golf, usually at the exclusive Bel-Aire Country Club, with its handsome course and show-business clientele. One member, the former Wimbledon tennis champion Bobby Falkenburg, himself a useful golfer, often played with the young Spaniard and steered him towards the Club's 'fat cats' – wealthy members who might one day sponsor Ballesteros on the tour.

In the evenings Ballesteros would dine simply with the Barners and then watch television, preferably old cowboy-and-Indian films. "We wanted to give Seve experience, and every time it got too much for him in Los Angeles we would get him out for three or four days," the American recalls. "We'd get him up to Cypress (Point), Pebble (Beach) and Spyglass Hill." These three courses, together with Monterey Country Club, form the glorious tournament sites on the Monterey Peninsula where, it was hoped, Ballesteros might one day succeed. When Franco died, and pictures were shown of the cortege passing through the streets of Madrid, Ballesteros sat alone in his room and wept.

He had been playing golf almost constantly now since early April, and his record for 1975 had taken a dramatic leap over that for the previous year. Not only was he top of both the Spanish and Continental Orders of Merit, but he had come 26th in the British, with five finishes within the top ten and an improved stroke average of 73.91 in thirteen counting tournaments. Still, his golfing work was not over for the year. In November he made his first trip to Japan, where he tied 17th in the Dunlop Phoenix, and a week later he appeared in his first World Cup, in Bangkok, where he and Angel Gallardo came 17th for Spain. Ballesteros had now been nearly two full years as a professional. "I had seen many good players for the first time in my life," he later recalled. "I thought to myself, 'Seve, you can beat them all.'"

Choosing Your Clubs

The first set of golf clubs I 'endorsed' were those 'Super' clubs mentioned in the last chapter. I was loyal, maybe too loyal, to them. The problems which they caused, which you will see in the next chapter, illustrate the fact that you should select the correct set of tools after you grow out of 1-club golf.

My first tip, maybe an obvious one, is that you must be comfortable with your clubs. If they don't immediately feel right, and even *look* right, the moment you pick them up, you probably have the wrong clubs. It is very rare that a player 'gets used to' or 'grows into' clubs. Like your clubs from the very beginning.

Woods: My English club maker Tom Gamble has an interesting theory. He thinks that players subconsciously are happiest playing the same coloured woods they first used as a boy or girl. Maybe this is true, I don't know.

But it is worth considering. He also has theories about why I like a black head on my woods. He says it not only is because my hair is jet black – Nicklaus and Miller use light-coloured woods – but, more interesting, black gives me a feeling of power. He says a black club also *looks* smaller and therefore gives a feeling of more power in relation to its weight. I think these ideas are true. But whether or not black suits you is something you must discover.

Club weight: Always remember, control your club; don't let your club control you. I think the mistake most players, especially amateurs, make is that their clubs are too heavy. I tell you, if a club feels heavy, the ball will go *nowhere*. That's all I have to say on this topic.

Shafts: If your swing is fast, the shaft should be stiff. If your swing is slow, your shaft should be more whippy. Mostly, I think amateurs choose shafts that are too whippy.

Grips: The bigger your hands, the bigger should be the grip. This is not surprising but amateurs don't always keep this in mind. I think, on the whole, people choose grips that are too small and this makes them hook the ball.

Irons: These clubs, like the woods, are a matter of taste and, I think, should suit your personality. For myself, I do not like a fussy head on my irons; just a simple shape with lots of rounded corners. When I look down the shaft of my irons, I like to get the feeling, which I am told is an illusion, that the leading edge of the blade is in line with the leading edge of the shaft.

The Sand Wedge: The standard sand wedge has a bulge below the leading edge of the blade; that is, when you rest it on the floor, the edge sets above the ground. This is supposed to make it easier to play out of sand. My sand wedge, however, has no bulge; the leading edge lies flat. I think players, especially in Britain, should try this design for two reasons: 1) it is easier to cut through all but the fluffiest of sand and, maybe more important, 2) it gives you another club and by that I mean another chipping iron for use round the greens.

The Putter: I am leaving this club, the most important one in the bag to the last because it will be the first specific club I will discuss. There are all sorts of putters, as you know, and simply choose the one that feels most comfortable. My advice is to take one where you can 'see the direction' off the face, that is one that gives you a clear sense of lining it up square. Finally, for what it is worth, I use a ping-style putter, weighted at the toe and the heel, because the way I play, with lots of long shots into the greens, I have many long putts to play. I find that if I mis-hit a putt with such a putter I will still get distance. Finally, 'feel' and 'comfort' are the key words in selecting a putter.

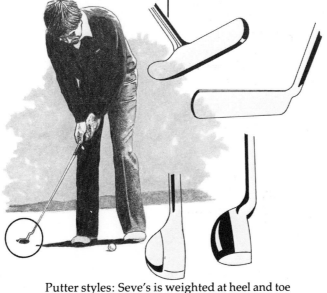

Putter styles: Seve's is weighted at heel and toe

CHAPTER THREE

THE SHOT HEARD ROUND THE WORLD

"I wish I could drive like you, Mr. Palmer."
"I wish I could putt like you, son."

Ballesteros and Arnold Palmer, playing together in
the Lancome Trophy, 1976, in Paris.

The Pedreña farmhouse was to become more and more cramped over the next three years, a cycling machine and ten sets of golf clubs replacing the cows and pigs in the basement. Trophies, cups and crystalware filled the sitting-room shelves and overflowed into Seve's bedroom where, in the far wall, a window was opened to the world.

In that time, from the ages of 18 through 21, Seve moved nearer to his mother's prophecy that one day he would become the world's greatest golfer. He three times won the Vardon Trophy, awarded annually to the winner of the British Order of Merit, and replaced Oosterhuis who in turn had replaced Jacklin as the finest player in Europe. He won eighteen tournaments in thirteen countries, including two World Cup team titles for Spain, and struck a number of outlandish shots from which legends were born. His genius was acknowledged, indeed heralded, by figures such as Nicklaus, Palmer, Trevino, Miller, Weiskopf and Player. "It is simple enough," Player said in those days; "he's the best young player in the world."

Still, by common consent Ballesteros's chief achievement during that period was not a tournament triumph: it was finishing second to Miller in the 1976 Open championship at Royal Birkdale, near Southport, in England. Miller knew the Spaniard's game well and saw parallels. "We both like to tee up the ball," he said. "Keep our heads still and let

it rip." Yet Miller took a more circumspect view of championship golf in Britain. "You need patience over here," he said. "You have to take bounce and roll into consideration on these seaside courses. You can't throw everything straight at the pin."

Ballesteros wasn't having such pre-championship nonsense. "I am still young," scoffed the 19-year-old, speaking then only in Spanish. "When I am older there will be time to be careful." He then went out and took Birkdale by the throat, threw *everything* at the pin, missed his mark often enough, scrambled over and round the mighty dunes, in and out of the willow scrub, and at the end of each of the first three days was leading the field.

On the last day, paired with and holding a two-stroke lead over Miller, the Spaniard was eager to get going. He played erratically, lost the lead for good by the sixth green and, dropping five strokes shortly after the turn, looked absolutely blown out of the championship.

But the Spaniard had not given up. He picked up four shots over the next five holes, including an eagle on the long 17th, and came to the last tee still hungry for more. Birkdale's finishing hole, a par 5 of 513 yards, was eminently birdieable. A par 5, the Spaniard reckoned, would keep him level with the American Ray Floyd in third place; a birdie and he would share second with Nicklaus. Ballesteros let rip with a gigantic drive into the light rough and followed it with an equally big long-iron that finished out of sight but up near the green.

Ballesteros was then to play what he would consider for years to be the most im-

The shot heard round the world: the only existing photograph of the delicate little pitch into the last green of the 1976 Open championship at Royal Birkdale that in the view of experts from Lee Trevino to John Jacobs set the young Spaniard apart from other golfers. Gary Halberg, the 1980 American Rookie of the Year, saw it on television and years later said he often thought of this shot while he battled against famous players.

---

portant stroke of his life. It was a shot literally heard round the world. Lee Trevino, nursing a damaged back, saw it on television at his home in Texas and later recalled letting out a loud Mexican whoop at its audacity. The British teaching professional, John Jacobs, was stunned by the courage exhibited by the shot. Jacobs, who had left Birkdale to watch the final round on TV at his Hampshire home, recalls, ''That shot alone convinced me that Seve was a genius. There wasn't another man in the field who would have attempted it.''

Ballesteros's ball lay in threadbare rough, to the left and short of the green. Some fifteen yards away a hard path, about two feet wide, humped between two bunkers and ran into the slippery green. The flag stood about seven yards into the green and beyond it the green drifted into oblivion. A firm wind was at his back. It would be a ticklish shot, no matter how the Spaniard chose to play it.

Seve looked at the scoreboard, and did his sums. He needed a chip and two putts to stay level with Floyd. He looked at his shot. I can play a sand wedge, high and safe, over the bunkers, he told himself. But if I do that I will never stop the ball, especially with this wind behind me. It may roll on and on and finish so far from the hole I'll need three putts to get down. Playing safe, he concluded, wasn't all that safe.

Ballesteros glanced again at the score board: a chip and *one* putt would give him a birdie and the second-place tie with Nicklaus. I can play a low 9-iron, keeping it under the wind, he reasoned, and bounce it just below the crest of the hump. If perfectly played, the ball will roll slowly into the pin. The dangers of playing this delicate little chip were obvious: if he fluffed the shot, or if the ball kicked left or right off the hard path, it would finish in a bunker. The Spaniard did not consider the consequences of such a result.

Ballesteros stopped his caddy from drawing the sand wedge from the bag. "Give me the 9-iron," he said. "We're going between the bunkers. If we make it, we make it." Years later, he estimated that his chances of making it were about one in ten but, at the time, he was convinced he could bring it off. He spent only a moment over the ball. *Slow,* he thought, and setting his jaw drew back his club head and struck the ball. It nipped up, dropped on to the path, skipped up the hump and crept down the slippery green.

Perfect, thought the Spaniard, the ball's going to stop short of the pin. It crept on and on and Ballesteros felt a flicker of panic before it finally came to rest about four feet past the flag. A quiet moment passed before the amphitheatre of fans surrounding the green burst into shouts and cheers. He holed the putt – it would have been an unthinkable anticlimax had he missed it – and finished second with Nicklaus. Ballesteros raised his hand to the acclaim but in fact he felt frustrated. He said to himself: I should have won this championship.

After the prize-giving ceremonies Miller sat long in the press tent and, although it was his hour, he heaped generous praise on the Spaniard. Ballesteros wouldn't buckle under pressure. Ballesteros would have won the championship had he used a 1-iron rather than a driver off more tees. He compared Ballesteros's failure to win with his own failure in the 1971 US Masters when, four holes from home, he had victory in sight and

let it slip. "As I look back I'm glad I didn't win that Masters," he said. "I wasn't ready. I feel the same for Seve. If he had won people would have put too much pressure on him. No, I think the best thing for his career was to finish second. His day will come."

Ballesteros's day came soon. Three weeks later he crushed all before him to win the Dutch Open at Zandvoort by three strokes. It was his first international victory yet his caddy, the Englishman Dave Musgrove, recalls his strange reaction. "What struck me then, and still does, is that he didn't bat an eyelid," says Musgrove. "It was as though he were born to win. Win once and there he was, teeing up next week as though he had never won in his life."

In another fortnight's time, Ballesteros ran away from the other seven men in the field in the Donald Swaelens Memorial trophy, bludgeoning the par 73 Royal Waterloo layout in Belgium with rounds of 67 and 68 to take a six-shot lead over Player going in to the final round of the 54-hole tournament. As at Birkdale, there was a key shot in this tournament, one that added to his list of outrageous shots.

On the second hole Ballesteros hooked his tee shot into a thick stand of trees near the green. Player, playing first from the fairway, chipped dead to the pin for a certain birdie. Ballesteros, facing a disastrous two-, even three-stroke swing, surveyed his shot. He was 45 yards from the flag but, crouching, he saw a line to it through a small gap in the trees, about head high and ten yards from his ball. He selected a 5-iron – the club with the proper loft to send a ball through the gap – and firmly punched his shot. The ball flew neatly through the gap, pitched ten yards short of the green, bobbled up and ran straight into the hole for an eagle two where, moments before, he was looking at catastrophe. "It was lucky the shot went in, yes," Ballesteros recalls, "but it was the sort of shot I learned to play as a boy with my 3-iron at Pedreña."

The following week it was Palmer's turn to feel the Spaniard's sting when, after three rounds of the Lancome trophy at St. Nom-

la-Breteche, near Paris, the two were at the top of the eight-man field. Ballesteros was confident and, to the alarm of his brother, Baldomero, he composed his winner's speech in his hotel room on the eve of the last day. Palmer, then 47 years old, was past his peak but he still had the fight, and the following. Before what at the time was the largest golf gallery ever assembled on the Continent, Arnie stormed through the first nine holes in two under par on the final day, opening up a four-stroke lead on the Spaniard.

It looked over, but Ballesteros kept his nerve. On the tenth, he holed a long, saving putt for a par. Still four strokes divided the two. On the eleventh, both had pars. On the twelfth, a long one, Ballesteros and Palmer exchanged compliments about each other's respective driving and putting and, heartened by the feeling of equality, Ballesteros picked up a birdie. Three strokes back. On the short thirteenth, the Spaniard holed a long birdie putt. Two back. At that moment, Seve said later, he was certain he could catch his rival.

The crunch came on the fifteenth when Ballesteros holed a 10-foot birdie putt to draw level. "Out of the corner of my eye I saw Palmer lowering his eyes and shaking his head," he recalls. "I knew his morale was gone and that made me feel good." *Made me feel good.* If the words sound cold-blooded, they are, for years later Ballesteros still savoured the satisfaction of crushing a player who once was an idol. "If you ever feel sorry for somebody on a golf course, you better go home," he said, with a grin and clench of his fist. "If you don't kill them, they'll kill you."

With yet another birdie, on the seventeenth, Ballesteros overtook Palmer to achieve the most stunning victory of his career to date. Palmer remembered it years later. "I hit nine greens on that back nine," he recalled, shaking his head as he must have done on that 15th green near Paris. "A lot of young guys might have got flustered in that situation, but the kid stayed cool. He shot five birdies on the back nine, didn't make a single mistake, scored a 31, and beat me by a stroke. I had heard he was tough but I didn't know he was that tough."

This hard competitive edge, sharpened by the Spanish *norteno's* natural suspicion, unsettles some American players. They don't know what to make of it. It was in such a climate that in the autumn of 1976 two incidents occurred that soured relations between Ballesteros and the Americans, a relationship that was to be further damaged by Ballesteros's disqualification from the 1980 US Open championship.

The first incident took place at Wentworth, near London, in October, in the week between Ballesteros's victories in the Swaelens and Lancome tournaments. The occasion was the Piccadilly World Match Play

championship, an eight-man tournament devised by – and some would say, for the benefit of – Mark McCormack, the American golfing agent whose players that year filled five of the eight places. When Ballesteros was drawn against the holder, Hale Irwin, then perhaps the finest match player in the game after Player, he was suspicious of the draw. Moreover, he was dubious over the prospect of playing face-to-face against another player rather than against an inanimate object, namely a golf course. For his part, Irwin, schooled in the traditional Rules of Golf, was unhappy with a new British PGA ruling, introduced that season, whereby grass torn up by shoe spikes could be tapped down on the greens.

What was more, heavy rain had recently fallen at Wentworth and accordingly players were allowed to pick their balls from the fairway, clean off the mud and replace the clean ball on the turf before playing again. Irwin found all this unsatisfactory for a tournament of such prestige and, feeling that the Spaniard was taking advantage of these rules through the morning round, at lunchbreak he complained to the referee, the former British Walker Cup player Ian Caldwell. "Watch Ballesteros closely this afternoon," Irwin said. "He's been fixing pitch marks, not spike marks." Caldwell was not aware of Seve having committed any infringement but when, on the first afternoon tee, a PGA official, Tony Gray, explained again the British rule to both players, the Spaniard felt his honour was under attack.

The players resumed battle in silence, the American suspicious and the Spaniard resentful. By the time they reached the 16th, or

Airforce volunteer Ballesteros. At £2 a week he taught golf to Spanish Air Force officers at their own golf course in the suburbs of Madrid. Fierce pride kept him from sitting an Army entrance examination for he distrusted any school. "I will not go through any examination whatsoever," he told Jorge de Ceballos with remarkable vehemence. "Not even through the US Qualifying School that the Americans want me to do. I have nothing to prove in golf and I do not regret not having as much culture as other people. I shall learn my own way through life."

34th, green Irwin was 1-up. Ballesteros had a 10-foot putt to square the match. A shoe mark dented his path to the hole. Ballesteros asked Irwin's permission to repair it. Irwin called in the referee and Caldwell, inspecting the mark closely, declared that no blades of grass were torn up by a shoe spike; play on. Ballesteros putted. His ball bobbled across the green and missed the hole.

The Spaniard, still 1-down and seething with rage on the next tee, snapped his drive out of bounds. He conceded the hole, lost the match 2 and 1, and set out for Paris to spend his rage on such luckless rivals as Palmer in the Lancome trophy.

The second incident, one of more lasting rancour, took place early in December at Palm Springs, California. The occasion was the World Cup. Ballesteros, with Manuel Piñero, represented Spain. The United States's pair was Jerry Pate, the reigning US Open champion, and Dave Stockton, who that summer had captured the US PGA championship. Spain and the US were paired on the second day and on the sixth hole, which plays over a ten-acre lake, both Spaniards hit long second shots which came to rest just off the green, dangerously close together.

Piñero's ball was plainly in the way of Ballesteros's swing. Under Rule 24 of the game Pinero was allowed to lift his ball but, under Rule 23, he was not allowed to clean it or have it cleaned by his caddy. The little Spaniard gave the ball to his caddy who received it in a towel. "One stroke penalty," Pate called out but the referee, uncertain whether or not the ball actually had been cleaned, refused to call such a penalty. Pate and Stockton protested and on the next tee Pate carried on with the argument that Piñero's 'black caddy' had cleaned the ball.

Pate is a Southerner. Piñero, from a humble background, is a player with a deep social conscience and he took Pate's words as a racial slur on his caddy. Tightening his lips, Piñero birdied the following hole. Pate dropped shots on each of the following three holes. Ballesteros added an eagle on the ninth and the Spaniards stormed to a three-stroke lead by the end of the day.

When, two days later, they went on to win the Cup for Spain, 474 strokes to 476 for the United States, Ballesteros burst into tears and fell into Piñero's arms. Spaniards thundered out of the crown across the wooden bridge to the island green and, for once, a Spanish television team was there to capture a golfing triumph. The Americans had been beaten on their own soil which, Spanish television viewers were reminded, was as likely as a second division Spanish football team winning the FA Cup at Wembley. For the Americans, the visitors' victory would forever be spoiled by the incident of the second day.

His part in the team title brought to a close a marvellous season for Ballesteros. When he came top of the British Order of Merit – for the first of three successive seasons – he was the first Continental to do so since the Belgian Flory van Donck in 1953. Ballesteros was also named Spanish sportsman of the Year by El Mundo *deportivo de Barcelona* but was still little known by the Spaniard in the street.

In the winter of early 1977 he was to serve his country in a more literal sense, as a private in the military service. A conscripted serviceman, under Spanish law, must serve twenty months, whereas a volunteer might choose where to go. A volunteer, however, must be armed with his primary school *certificado*; Ballesteros had none. Out of pride, he refused to sit such a rudimentary examination for the Army and, after a prolonged and anxious stalemate, the authorities relented and turned a blind eye for such a dignitary. At a salary of £2 a week, Ballesteros served his time in Madrid, much of it giving exhibitions and teaching the niceties of golf to Air Force officers.

In April of 1977 Spain's most famous private was given extended 'leave' to accept an invitation to play in his first US Masters. Seve's performances at Augusta are the subject of another section of this book, but for the moment, one aspect of the 1977 Masters is worthy of note. He was respected, even before the place laid eyes on him. In fact, so world-renowned was the Spaniard – the biggest teenage golfing celebrity since Bobby Jones – that the distinguished American magazine *Golf Digest* blazed him across its cover, with the legend, "Can this teenager win the Masters?"

Through all this clamour of publicity Ballesteros kept his head. A charming story is told, for instance, of him stopping soon after at a soft drinks shack during the Spanish Under-25s professional championship. "I have the same surname – 'Ballesteros' – as you," said the attendant, all afluster. Ballesteros, in reply, asked him his age and when the man said twenty-nine, Ballesteros smiled. "I am only twenty-one," he replied, "so in that case you do not have the same name as me; *I* have the same name as *you*."

Ballesteros did splendidly by himself that year, spreading his wings to win eight international tournaments, from the French Open in May through to two victories in Japan, including their Open Championship, and on through New Zealand into the Philippines where in December he joined with Antonio Garrido to capture another World Cup team title for Spain. Not since Byron Nelson, Ben Hogan and Sam Snead has anyone won so often in a year; *no one* had ever won in seven different countries.

In 1978 Ballesteros went from strength to strength. He won seven titles in as many countries, from Kenya through Europe and on into the United States and Japan. In a stretch of six summer weeks in Europe he sustained his brilliance for a longer period of time than he would do for years. Given six fewer strokes, strategically placed in that period, the Spaniard would have won all six of those tournaments. As it was he won three, came second twice and returned 20 out of 23 rounds under par.

Ballesteros was without question a great player and other great ones began acknowledging the fact. Trevino called Ballesteros a golfer who comes only once in a generation. Nicklaus said after Ballesteros came joint-18th at Augusta in 1978, "He won't win just one Masters' jacket. He will win many, of that I'm sure. He has everything that's needed." Tom Weiskopf's observation was simpler, perhaps more pertinent. "Seve," he said, "is the most

The big shot: Ballesteros, having just completed his famous drive over the water and into the tenth green (*right*) at the Belfry in 1978. His opponent, Nick Faldo, has his mouth open in surprise. Notice also the scoreboard: in 1978 the Belfry was one of the first courses in Britain to mark the distances of their holes metrically.

exciting player I've seen since Arnold Palmer.''

The excitement of Ballesteros, like that of Palmer, took its form in raw power and unpredictability, the capacity to save himself from disaster after willingly courting it. It is rare enough for a golfer to be remembered for single audacious shots – as Jones, Sarazen,

The champions: in a Madrid restaurant Seve, *second from left*, dines with the Mexican golfer, Ernesto Perez Acosta, shortly after Acosta won the individual World Cup title and Ballesteros contributed to the team title in 1976. With them are Mili Ceballos and Jorge Ceballos, Seve's advisor, and, *right*, Pedro Morán, a childhood friend from Pedreña.

Hogan, Palmer had been through their careers – but for a player so young to have built up such a number of them was remarkable. For power, for instance, there was the way he played the eighteenth at Cologne, on the way to winning the 1978 German Open. The hole, measuring 594 yards, is one of the longest in tournament golf and, having himself reached the green in two big wood shots and a healthy pitch, Gary Player asked Ballesteros how he had handled the monster hole.

The Spaniard had reached, indeed was *through* the green with a drive and a 3-wood. "Can you believe that?" Player later told his agent, Mark McCormack. "The Ballesteroses

of this world will be shooting regularly in the fifties in years to come. Thank goodness I've got my titles won."

The shot of the year in 1978, at least on the European side of the Atlantic, was played at The Belfry, the British PGA's dreary home course at Sutton Coldfield. It came during Ballesteros's match against England's Nick Faldo in the Hennessy Cup between Great Britain and Ireland and the European Continent. The far end of the fairway of the tenth, par 4 and 310 yards, nips sharply right behind a tall stand of trees and over a small lake, beyond which sits the green. Faldo, one down but playing first, struck an easy, conventional iron from the tee, leaving himself a pitch over the water.

Ballesteros and Musgrove discussed the shot: the wind, blowing left to right, would help an ambitious fade round the trees and over the water but, slightly against it, it would hold up the necessary all-carry drive into the green. Whichever way he cut it, any attempt at driving the green would require a massive blow. The Spaniard, reckoning he could break his opponent by doing so, finally asked for his driver: his towering drive, tailing off round the trees, settled down twenty feet short of the hole, checked and ran perhaps ten feet. Ballesteros thinks the drive carried 284 yards, a phenomenal shot and, although he missed the eagle putt, he took a 3 and went on to win the match, 2 and 1.

If that delicately-weighted little pitch into the last green of the 1976 Open at Birkdale was the finest shot Ballesteros played through the early part of his career and the drive at Belfry the boldest and most dramatic, his victory in the Greater Greensboro Open early in 1978 was certainly his most important triumph. It was a seminal occasion coming, as it did, in America. It was not, however, a victory of the highest merit, as Seve admitted. "I was very, very lucky," he says. "I don't know how I win the tournament."

For a start, the field was weak. Nicklaus, Watson, Irwin, Trevino and others were away, preparing for the Masters, to be played the following week. The Spaniard's opening rounds of 72 and 75 left him at the bottom of the field, ten strokes behind the leader; but as back-marker he was the first man to tee off on the third day which, in retrospect, was a blessing in disguise. He had nearly finished his third round when a galloping wind swept down the course, kicking up worse and worse as the leaders neared the home hole. As a result, Ballesteros's 69 was the best score of the day, and left him only five strokes off the pace.

Lanny Wadkins, who has often played with Ballesteros, was the Spaniard's playing partner in the final round. "I was in a position to win, too, and we both played well," recalls Wadkins, then the reigning US PGA champion. In the event Ballesteros, with a final round of 66, won the title by a single stroke. "I remember him going through the front nine about five under par," Wadkins recalls. "What was strange was that all his birdies came from really long putts, thirty or forty feet. He was marvellous to watch. Some guys have got stone hands; Seve's are light as a feather. Anyway, on the tenth he drove the ball perfectly down the fairway. He followed that with a beautiful 7-iron that finished three feet behind the hole. And then he missed the putt. Jesus, he was cooking! I reckoned he had had it, but two holes later he turned around and holed from about forty feet for a birdie. He's amazing in that respect. The misses don't bother him. There is nobody quite like him – although, I must admit, it's hard to tell what's going on inside."

The triumph, Seve's first in the United States, set American journalists thumbing through their record books. Never before had the midway back-marker rushed up through the field to win a tour tournament; Ballesteros was the first foreign non-tour member to win an American event since the South African Harold Henning won the Texas Open in 1966. In American golf history, only three times had there been younger winners than the Spaniard, exactly a week short of his 21st birthday: Gene Sarazen was 20 years 4 months old when he won the 1922 US Open; Horton Smith 20 years five months when he took the 1928 Oklahoma City Open and Raymond Floyd 20 years six months at the time he captured the 1963 St. Petersburg Open.

It should have come as no surprise that Deane Beman, US PGA Tour Commissioner, bowed to pressure from sponsors and offered Ballesteros a 'card' to join the US tour and gave him sixty days to consider the offer. Nor was it surprising that the following week, after completing his second round of the Masters, the Spaniard found a letter in his Augusta locker. It was an invitation for him to play in the United States PGA championship later in the summer at Oakmont. "As you know, you are the first foreign player ever to have received such an official exemption in the history of the PGA championship," declared the letter. "We are happy to extend this to you on behalf of the PGA Executive Committee."

Ballesteros, mistakenly advised by Barner the US PGA was not a major event, gracefully declined both the invitation to the championship and the 'card' offer from Beman. He had commitments elsewhere, he explained. "Besides," he said privately, "I had already been in the Army and playing on the American tour is like being in the Army. You always have to ask the Captain for permission to visit somewhere else in the world."

In the world of golf, Ballesteros was moving into a vacuum left by what was, at the time, thought to be the imminent decline of Nicklaus and the colourful Trevino. And, after a long hiatus, the Press was on the look-out for a new Palmer. Jim Murray, the witty sports columnist of the *Los Angeles Times*, wrote: "He goes after a golf course like a lion at a zebra. He doesn't reason with it; he tries to throw it out of the window or hold its head under water till it stops wriggling."

In action: the power and emotion that has made Ballesteros the most exciting golfer since Palmer.

Getting to Grips with the Game

Pick up your club, any one of your clubs. Grip it. No, that's wrong! Almost certainly, you're holding your club too tight. If your grip is tight you may feel more powerful but look, the muscles of your forearms are tight – and this means you will not be able to make any speed in your swing. Golf needs club-head speed. So, first, you must always grip the club gently. Peter Dobereiner, of the London *Observer*, once asked me to hold his forefinger in my normal grip. "The pressure," he wrote, "would not have squeezed toothpaste from the tube." Now, the type of grip. Of the two most common ways of holding a club, the overlapping or interlocking grip, I prefer the overlap because the interlocking grip, I think, stops the free movement of the fingers and wrists. And one last word about the grip: many professionals feel that amateurs should use 'stronger' grips, that is grips with the right hand rolled more over the shaft. I disagree. I think a too-strong grip makes you hook and makes it harder to control distance.

Set-up: The most important thing in the set-up is to be comfortable, something some people forget, because you will never make a good swing if you are not comfortable. Try many stances until you find your own individual style: more open, more closed, knees bent, head a little behind the ball. Practise and try to relax; and again, make sure you're comfortable.

The Kick-off: Every action has an exact moment when it starts and, in golf, I think you should signal it with a small movement, maybe a little cock of the knee, a waggle of the club or a forward push with the hands. My own pre-swing movement is to press the head of the club slightly into the ground and, at the same time, press my wrists a little lower in the grip. These little starting movements focus your concentration.

The Swing: Start the backswing with both hands and with the left shoulder, left hip and left knee all moving together. Bring the club a few inches straight back and as you turn, the hips should turn as much as they can without moving the right knee. As your backswing nears the top, your wrists should cock naturally – *don't think about cocking them* – and, finally, practise until it comes natural that your clubhead at the top of the backswing points *exactly at the target*. Sometimes, you will find that you must start the backswing a little bit from the 'inside' to get the clubhead pointing this way at the target. And, in the downswing, the one thing you must remember is to accelerate on impact; your fastest clubhead speed should be at the moment you hit the ball.

Rhythm: This is the most important thing in the golf swing, both in the irons and the woods. For example, if you want to hit a long drive, you swing with rhythm – one-two – and don't try to swing fast. Instead, make a longer swing and take the hands further back, and then by slowing down the swing you make it possible to speed up the hands through impact.

The Grip: Seve uses the over-lap, with the right hand down the shaft

CHAPTER FOUR

VOICES: PREPARING FOR THE 1979 OPEN

"This boy, he serious. If he want to go to Glasgow, he go to Glasgow — and he not stop on the way."

Roberto de Vicenzo

The sun stood high and clouds hurried inland as a chill breeze carried the tang of the Irish sea across the Lancashire coast of England. It was about noon on 21 July, 1979, the final day of the 108th Open championship at Royal Lytham and St. Annes and, by now, most of the players were out on the links. The home green was empty, waiting. A silver trophy, glittering on a table behind it, could be seen through the locker room window of the clubhouse. From within, the attendant beckoned to the lone golfer behind him. "Come over and have a look," he said. "Isn't it beautiful?"

The golfer, Ballesteros, joined him to gaze at the trophy which later in the day would be presented to the champion. It looked odd, exotic on a table that tilted in a garden-party setting of freshly mown grass. As he gazed, Ballesteros presented a striking figure in his dark blue sweater and trousers, white shoes and white shirt opened at the throat. He is an uncommonly intense man, and his brooding air, enhanced by his dark complexion and high cheekbones, can frighten even his friends.

Wearing that brooding look, Ballesteros returned to the bench by his locker. He sat down and dropped his head into his hands. Although a Virgin Mary medallion dangled from his neck, Ballesteros is *catolico non fanatico*, a believer but not a practising Catholic. He was surprised therefore to find that for the first time in his life he was praying for help in winning a golf tournament. "I did not pray to play well," he later recalled. "I prayed to *win* – because I knew it was possible. '*Padre nuestro . . .*'"

Victory certainly was possible; but to achieve it he had a fight on his hands. After three rounds he lay in second place, sandwiched between two strong, reigning champions; Hale Irwin, winner a month earlier of the US Open, and the Open holder Jack Nicklaus, who the previous summer had captured the championship at St. Andrews. Otherwise, with the exception of the American Ben Crenshaw, the leaderboard looked only moderately formidable:

> Irwin, 211.
> Ballesteros, 213.
> Nicklaus, 214.
> Mark James, Britain, 214
> Crenshaw, US, 215
> Roger Davis, Australia, 215
> Bob Byman, US, 215

Into Seve's mind came the spectre of the last good chance he had had at the Open: at Birkdale in 1976 when he had gone into the last round, two shots in front, only to lose to Johnny Miller. *Coming second*, Miller had said afterwards, *will give him just that bit more time to prepare himself for winning a big one.*

This time Ballesteros was prepared. In

fact, he had never been better prepared for a tournament in his life. In the previous fortnight, after missing the cut in the US Open at Inverness in Toledo, Ballesteros had won the English Classic at the British PGA's headquarters at The Belfry, hammering out a six-stroke victory over the tediously long Midlands layout, and then finished second after a keen duel with the Briton Sandy Lyle in the Scandinavian Open at Helsingborg, Sweden.

He had come early to Lytham, knowing little more about the course than what he had learned one afternoon during the Spanish Open many weeks before when his caddy showed him a booklet containing diagrams of each of the holes. Ballesteros had remarked on the great number of bunkers on the course and Musgrove, who had already worked there as a caddy in three Opens, replied that there were said to be 365, one for each day of the year. Great bunker players, Musgrove said, always won at Lytham: Player, Jacklin, Charles and Thomson and, earlier, Locke and the great Bobby Jones. It was an observation calculated to encourage Ballesteros, much as Musgrove's remark three years earlier that the Spaniard would like Birkdale for its par 5 holes. And of Lytham Ballesteros had responded accordingly: "No problem, I am the best bunker player." The Spaniard's remark was to weather well, for his deft sand play, more than his much-reported escapes from remote places, was to be a hallmark of his play throughout the championship.

Apart perhaps from those plentiful bunkers, Lytham, the northernmost of the famed Lancashire links, is not especially noted for any single feature. It is the most unprepossessing of the championship links and, if one applies the common definition of 'links' as seaside duneland, it is not a links at all. The course is half a mile from and out of sight of the sea, bounded on one side by the

Royal Lytham & St. Annes Golf Club – the scene of Ballesteros's 1980 Open championship victory. The opening three holes are strung up the right, alongside the railway lines, and the home green lies inside the bunkers at the bottom-centre of the photograph.

Blackpool-Preston railway line and on the others mostly by dour, red brick Edwardian houses.

Flat, unspectacular, Lytham's strength lies in the fact that among its eighteen holes there is not one easy 'breather'; they each offer a stern challenge. In 1910 Bernard Darwin described the lay-out in his book *The Great Golf Courses of the British Isles*. His words still apply:

". . . St. Anne's is very smooth and trim, and just a little artificial. If the day is calm and we are hitting fairly straight, the golf seems rather easy than otherwise; and yet we must never allow ourselves to think so too pronouncedly, or we shall straightaway find it becoming unpleasantly difficult. If there is a strong wind blowing we shall not even be tempted to think it easy, for there is plenty of rough grass on either side, and the hitting of a good straight tee-shot, which seemed so simple and made the holes seem simple, will be a cause of considerable anxiety. Whatever the weather and the wind, there is one thing that we ought always to do well at St. Anne's, and that is putt, for the greens are as good and true as any in the world . . ."

It wasn't until 1926, however, that Lytham joined the championship rota. And who better than the great Bobby Jones could have been chosen to win Lytham's inaugural championship?

"Model your game on Bobby Jones's," a young South African, Bobby Locke, was being told at the time by his father, and it was Locke who was to win Lytham's next Open, in 1957. The championship returned to Lytham in 1969 when Tony Jacklin, aged 26, became the first of his countrymen in eighteen years to win it. And most recently Ballesteros's idol, Gary Player, had won at Lytham in 1974.

For her part, Spain never had provided a championship finisher higher than Ballesteros's runner-up result in 1976, although her golfers had long competed in the championship. They commonly practised together and, at least in recent years, joked, swapped advice and, in moments of unbridled horse-play, even swatted each others' balls into the rough. Ballesteros had long ago foregone such a lackadaisical approach. For this reason he rarely practised with Spain's other two leading players, Manuel Piñero and Antonio Garrido. "This boy, he serious," the Argentine Roberto de Vicenzo says of Seve. "He never fool around on a golf course."

De Vicenzo, who already had played in five of the six Lytham Opens, knew the vagaries of the course and when Seve arrived at Lytham on practice days in 1979 he was there, waiting for him on the putting green, quietly waiting to be asked to play: a relaxed trouper who made the younger player grin with affection. As at Birkdale in 1976, de Vicenzo was to shepherd Seve round on those practice days.

On the first day, Seve's brother, Manuel, who was also playing in the Open, joined the pair. Another brother, Vicente, caddied for Manuel and the third brother, Baldomero, tagged along. It was too much. De Vicenzo was not amused. "We made jokes that day because the other fellows look for jokes. But pretty soon one brother start telling Seve what he must do on one hole and another brother tell him what he must do on the next. It was no good. I had to say to Seve: 'Look, sometimes when you play you listen to too many voices. Listen only to the voice within your head.'"

Seve chose to listen to one other voice: de Vicenzo's. "Roberto is the master and I am the pupil," he says, "And I will use all the knowledge from his life." To begin with: what, overall, did Roberto think of Lytham? Roberto thought many things. First, he said, trouble at Lytham lay mainly to the right sides of the fairway; to avoid it Seve must draw the ball – that is, curve the flight from right to left. Second, he must gather good scores on the easier, outward, usually downwind nine holes which, at 3,298 yards, form the shortest

---

Ballesteros and Roberto de Vincenzo, the grand old man of Spanish-speaking golf, played practice rounds to learn the routes to success at Royal Lytham in 1979.

outward journey in British championship golf. Third, not least, when things went wrong Seve must be patient. There wasn't a tournament in the world that tried a player's patience like an Open, with its hard-baked fairways off which a ball might unexpectedly bounce left or right. Just as maddening was its weather, which might suddenly, and unfairly, change from good to bad during the day.

One day de Vicenzo left Ballesteros on the practice area and wandered out on to the course where he found Nicklaus playing serenely, followed by a sprinkling of fans. De Vicenzo watched the holder for a few holes and, much encouraged, returned to Ballesteros. "Look, Nicklaus is the man to beat here – and yet already he is playing too safe," he said. "He's going to wait for the other fellows to make the mistakes. You can't do that, because if you play safe, if *everybody* play safe, your chances will be the same as everybody else's. You must play different. You must forget everybody else and *hit* the ball."

De Vicenzo told Seve the course suited him better than any other championship course in Britain. "In front of the greens there are many bumps," he said, "and your high shot on to the green will be good. Also, you can hit *over* trouble here more than at any other Open course." De Vicenzo had observed that the Royal and Ancient Golf Club of St. Andrews organisers of the Open had worried more about making tee shots at Lytham difficult for the middle-distance hitters than the big hitters – players such as Nicklaus and Ballesteros. "There are many places outside the fairway that are not so bad, not so dangerous – if you hit it *long*. Out beyond 240-250 yards the rough in many places is thin and weak. You will see." These barren patches of rough were often, surprisingly, the legacy of old Opens, especially 'Jacklin's championship' of 1969, which had never recovered from the heavy trampling of galleries. "Seve beat us," Jim Arthur, the R and A

Seve during the 1979 Open, in typical dark-coloured clothing.

agronomist confessed after the championship. "We simply couldn't get some of those patches of rough to grow back."

In search of them, Ballesteros often drove two practice balls from each of the tees. On all but the short holes, where obviously he aimed for the putting surfaces, he knocked his first ball firmly towards traditional and conservative targets in the fairways, places that were not only free from rough, sand and uncertain footing but ones that 'opened' safe passages to the greens. It was then that the fun started. Ballesteros would unload his second drive with more power, looking for distant landing areas, far off the tees, that were covered by benign, 'weak' rough and reachable only by the longest and boldest of hitters.

He found them too. The fourteenth was an example. At first glance, it does not look to be one of Lytham's most challenging holes. At 445 yards it is a long par 4, yet it is reasonably straight and flat and the green remains in sight from anywhere on the passably

No man is a hero to his caddy: David Musgrove and Ballesteros, fighting friends, a marriage of two strong wills that didn't always work.

generous fairway. One's first glance is deceiving – as it often is on seaside links. It is a hole where, after he begins his crucial run for home, a player's nerve threatens to break. The hole is prey to a prevailing wind, left to right, which, up near the green, can blow a golfer's ball into the thickest of rough.

In the official Open programme for the year, Colin Maclaine, chairman of the championship committee and past captain of the Lytham club, set out the conventional wisdom about playing the course. "As to the fourteenth itself," wrote Maclaine, "the drive has to be a little leftish because of those obstructive humps down the right . . ." Those humps of which he speaks, covered with unruly grass, rise at about 230 and 270 yards from the tee.

Obstructive grassy humps or not, it was decided to send Ballesteros down that right side with one of his big, high drives; let his ball bounce into a patch of balding rough between the two humps. So it went, round the course, areas of distant thin rough upon which Ballesteros could draw his bead. Musgrove didn't bother to sketch these targets on his otherwise much-marked map of the course. "Once Seve plays a course he knows it," Musgrove says. "He has one of the best memories in golf."

De Vicenzo's plan had worked. On the opening three days of play, Ballesteros had missed fairways galore – in fact, only *eight* did he hit with drives – but he missed them on the thin-rough sides and suffered little. Yet on the first day, in a stiff and chilly breeze, his game was lacklustre. His score of 73 left him in joint-16th place, eight strokes behind the little-known Briton Bill Longmuir, and in the wake of those who on the final day would challenge him: Irwin returned a 68, Aoki a 70, Nicklaus and Crenshaw both 72.

On the second day the Spaniard played a round full of colour and controversy. Again in a cold breeze, his wild tee shots regularly finished in threadbare rough. This time, however, he holed a couple of long putts and played the outward nine holes splendidly in 33, two under par. Standing on the tenth tee his playing partner, Lee Trevino, spoke to

him in Spanish. The reason Ballesteros was driving so badly, the American said, was that he was not following through his swing on impact; he was blocking against his left leg. "After that," Ballesteros said later, "I played good." He played better than good; over what Nicklaus calls the toughest finishing run in British golf Ballesteros pried four birdie threes out of five holes. His astonishing homeward 32 earned him a 65.

The Spaniard was thus 138 at the midway point, two strokes behind Irwin, who returned another 68, a stroke clear of the fading Longmuir, and three ahead of Nicklaus, five of Crenshaw and six of Aoki. In the press tent after the round, however, Ballesteros was asked what he and Trevino, his playing partner, spoke of in Spanish. Ah, said Seve, innocent enough, Trevino passed along a tip. Those who heard this were startled. Clearly, the incident contravened Rule 9 (1) of the game which calls for a two-stroke penalty for

Ballesteros with Musgrove on the final day of the Open. "I once told Seve that some players get frightened and back off when they get into a position to win," Musgrove once recalled. "He didn't believe me. He just looked at me kind of funny."

"Giving or Asking for Advice. . . ." Strictly speaking Ballesteros had neither given nor requested advice and, if anyone faced a penalty, it was Trevino. The officials turned a blind eye to the infringement – as they had done nearly three decades earlier on the occasion of Locke's slow play.

On the previous day Ballesteros played alongside Irwin and, as the American put it: "We never seemed to have a handle on things." They each scored 75. A smart westerly breeze had sprung up, the approaches to the green had been unpredictably watered and a few of the other players found their handles. Nicklaus, for instance, scored 73, Watson 76. The Spaniard was left nestling neatly between Irwin and Nicklaus at the top of the leaderboard.

The night before Ballesteros had appeared in relaxed and happy mood at the Lytham house which had been rented for him for the duration of the championship. Seve was staying there with his brother, Baldomero, his friend and adviser, Jorge de Ceballos, as well as his American business managers, Barner and Collet, and the managers' wives.

Although Ballesteros neither sought nor received special privileges in the household he was given the only steak that evening when the lamb chops smelled faintly rancid. After dinner Collet double-checked that a car would arrive to whisk the Spaniard to the course on time. Ballesteros leafed through a golf magazine. He scarcely saw it, preoccupied. He stretched and lolled his head in a rotating motion and rolled over his wrists, as he often does, listening for the clicking.

Ballesteros soon slipped away to his bedroom. For a long time he lay unable to sleep. He was chiefly worried about the follow-through of his swing during the first three days and, in particular, the follow-through when he used such heavy artillery as the driver. His arms had come through straight out, wrists together, rather like a parody of Arnold Palmer or perhaps a bell-ringer being pulled off his feet. "It is a bad, bad swing," he muttered, over and over. He was convinced it was brought on by his bad back.

He tried to read. Ballesteros's tastes in literature run to golf magazines and Western penny-dreadfuls written in Spanish. "I like cowboy-and-Indian books, the kind John Wayne makes movies about," he says. "I read that night until I forgot about my problems and started worrying about the Indians."

Ballesteros was awake at 8 o'clock. On each of the three previous mornings he had visited a physiotherapist in Lytham for a massage of his troubled back and a swim in a pool. "I didn't go to the physiotherapist on the last morning," he recalls. "I didn't want the time of the appointment on my mind."

At the course, Ballesteros was greeted by well-wishers, including several socialite Spaniards, looking odd and elegant in their stylish forest-green cape-coats, and his first benefactor, Jose Santiuste from Santander. "You must win," Santiuste said softly. "And then give me the ball."

Ballesteros's tee-off time – 1.20 p.m. – was much on his mind and it was 12.30 when he left the locker room. The practice ground was all but empty: only the leading players, still to tee off, were there. Nicklaus was standing hands on hips, waiting for his caddy, Jimmy Dickinson, to pick over the balls lying far out on the ground. Dickinson was especially looking for balata-covered balls. In competition Nicklaus uses balls with balata covers, natural gutta percha, because with them he can shape his shots better than with balls covered with synthetic Surlyn. Although most top professionals use the balata-covered balls, few are so finicky as to refuse, as does Nicklaus, to practise with the synthetic kind.

Musgrove awaited Ballesteros. He was ready with the clubs: a conventional assortment comprising a driver, a 3-wood, the irons from 1 to 9, a sand wedge, a pitching wedge and a putter. The single curious aspect of the selection was that Ballesteros, after chopping and changing between two different drivers in the opening three rounds, had suddenly decided upon the first one again.

If fairly ordinary, Ballesteros's ritual on practice grounds is a thoughtful one. He plays himself in, loosening up by hitting about ten balls with his 8-iron. He hits about the same number with the stronger irons, the 6, the 4 and finally the 1-iron. He moves to the 3-wood for about ten shots and finally the driver for a dozen full-blooded blows. His work was now about to begin. He hit a dozen more shots with the 6-iron, for that would be the first club he would bring into battle.

The opening hole at Lytham, unlike any opener on any other major golf course, is a par 3, invariably buffeted by winds that one cannot read from the sheltered tee; and so presents a stern first challenge to the golfer. Ballesteros, wisely, prepared for this challenge on the practice putting green.

The legendary putters of golf – Bobby Locke, Bobby Jones, Billy Caspar, Bob Charles, Arnold Palmer in his prime – have almost to a man subscribed to the theory that a player must practise putting from short distances and, only as touch and confidence come, move out to longer and finally very long approach putts. Theoretically this is sound, but faced with Lytham's short first Ballesteros took a more pragmatic view. "On the first hole you are stiff and cold and a little nervous and, from the tee, it is hard to put the ball close to the flag," he explains. "So you must realise that you will probably put the ball far from the hole – and leave yourself a long putt. That is why I practised long putts, 20 to 30 feet, before I practised the short ones."

It was now 1.10 by Seve's wristwatch. On the way to the first tee he was surprised to find de Vicenzo standing in his path. Seve had thought the Argentinian, upon missing the halfway cut, had set out for home. "No, I stay to see you win," said de Vicenzo, clapping his young friend on the shoulder. *"Tienes las manos,"* he said, *"Ahora juega con tu corazon."* You have the hands, now you must play with your heart.

Playing in the Wind

At Royal Lytham and St. Annes, where I won the 1979 Open championship, the winds blow strong and gusty, as they do on all British seaside courses. They blow on the high open layout at Puerta de Hierro in Madrid, too, one of Spain's finest courses. In fact, everyone has to play in bad winds some days. So here are some tips for such conditions.

Don't waste time over the ball: Always remember that what the wind, especially a gusty wind, does to you is more important than what it does to the ball. Don't stand too long over the ball because the wind will move your body and ruin your stroke, whether it is a drive, an iron shot or a putt. My rule is to stand one step away from the ball, take my practice swings, then step up, grip the club just a little more tightly, settle in and hit the ball without wasting time.

Putting in the wind: I discuss putting elsewhere but, when putting in the wind, I hold the club a little tighter. Further, shorten your swing, backwards and forwards, and try to strike the ball firmly and solidly. Next, worry more about your distance than your direction; just try to run the ball up close. Finally, do not let the wind dictate the line of your putt; take command by hitting the ball aggressively.

Irons and Woods in the wind: The most difficult wind to play these shots in is one that blows from left to right because it will move your body over the ball, you will 'cut' it by swinging outside-in, and the sliced shot will go far out to the right. You can solve this problem in one of two ways: 1) aim out to the left and let the wind carry the ball towards the target or, more difficult, 2) take one extra club, try to aim it straight at the pin, keeping your right elbow in close to your side. This will tend to make you *hook* the ball into the target.

A right to left wind, on the other hand, is easier to play in. As the wind shifts you away from the ball in your stance, your swing becomes in-and-out and, therefore, you draw the ball to the left. A draw is easier than a fade to control in the wind; therefore, I aim far out to the right, maybe as much as 40 yards (if I'm using, say, full wood in a big wind) and ninety per cent of the time the ball will come back on to the target.

Stopping a ball downwind: This can be difficult but, remember, the better you hit it the better the ball stops. Don't ease up if the wind is at your back. Just take a loftier club.

Hitting low tee shots into the wind: In this case, tee up the ball further forward, maybe inside your left toe-cap, grip the club a little shorter down the shaft, make a three-quarter swing and hit it easy. The harder you hit a ball into the wind the higher it will soar and lose distance.

Wind: let it shape your shot to the target

CHAPTER FIVE

VICTORY AT LYTHAM

"That the winner, Severiano Ballesteros, chose not to use it [the course] but preferred his own, which mainly consisted of hay fields, car parks, grand stands, dropping zones and even ladies' clothing, was his affair. Nevertheless he was a very worthy Open Champion."

Colin Maclaine, Chairman of the Championship Committee, in recording gratitude to the Captain and Members of Royal Lytham and St. Annes Golf Club for the condition of their course during the 1979 Open Championship.

At the turn of the century Lytham and St. Annes golf course rose from marshy agricultural duneland alongside the Blackpool–Preston railway line. In the ensuing years the land was drained, leaving a handsome stand of willows near the railway line. The boughs of these willows, as well as the flags on the course, were tossing in the wind as Ballesteros arrived on the tee for the last day of the championship. The Spaniard, himself standing in a cloister of trees, took notice of the wind's direction by looking at the flags. He said hello all round: the scorekeeper, the referee, Irwin's caddy, Irwin himself . . . The American did not smile. Today Irwin will be cold to play with, Ballesteros said to himself; there will not be much laughter.

Irwin *was* cold. He stood, arms akimbo, wearing two sweaters and a scowl. He peered through thick steel-rimmed glasses at the foul British weather: if it rained his glasses would be sure to blur. Their blurring the previous day had cost him a double-bogie 6 on the seventeenth hole and a four-stroke lead. Also, deep in his mind, he was disturbed by being heckled the previous day while lining up a putt. "Miss it, Irwin . . . Go home, Yank!" His gloom would damage his chances – the American recognised that – but it would continue through the day. Hale, you've got to put your game together, he told himself. You've got to find the handle.

Ballesteros was in an altogether different frame of mind. He was uplifted by de Vicenzo's remark moments before – *you must play with your heart* – and he, too, felt cold. His chill, however, was one of anticipation, and it lay like a comforting lump in his stomach. He drew confidence from news brought back from the first green by his caddy: Nicklaus, the only golfer the Spaniard feared in the world, had dropped a shot. If he could get a birdie here, the Spaniard told himself, or on the second or third holes, he could win. Accordingly, these holes are worth closer study.

Hole One, 206 yards. Ballesteros bent to plunge his tee into the turf and, by habit, tossed the grass into the air as he rose. The grass fell straight down, signifying nothing. Still, from the trees and the flag, he could see the wind direction: right to left and mostly from behind. He chose the 7-iron rather than the 6 with which he had practised so long. He consulted Musgrove who checked a diagram of the first green in his coursebook: '24L', it read, which in caddy shorthand meant the pin was set 24 paces from the front, and in the left of the green. The Spaniard settled his feet and shoulders and – *swish*. Seve dropped his right shoulder, twisted. The ball obediently curved right, held up a bit against the wind, and plopped on to the green to come to rest fifteen feet to the right of the flag: a cunningly executed shot.

The American was uncertain of his club selection. The previous day his 6-iron had pitched just short of the green and skipped through it. He again chose his 6; again the ball dropped just short of the green but this time it reared up and trickled feebly on to the putting surface, far short of the flag. Irwin shook his head: typical, he thought; you can't trust bounces on British seaside courses.

As the entourage moved off the tee, Referee Behrend, deputy chairman of the championship committee, swallowed and prayed that over the next four hours he would not be called upon to make an awkward ruling. Ballesteros, walking beside his caddy, suddenly asked, "David, how many balls do we have?" Musgrove thought: it's a little late to ask that. "Two dozen," he replied. "And about fifty golf tees." And six new golf gloves, one of which Musgrove would soon, on instruction, put on; Seve preferred them broken-in before he wears them.

On the green, Ballesteros picked a line one inch to the right of the cup and stroked his ball firmly. It rumbled over the badly spike-marked green, turned at the last moment and plunged into the middle of the hole. The Spaniard had got what he wanted: a birdie 2. Irwin two-putted for a par, and Ballesteros, now a single stroke behind, led the way towards the second tee.

Hole Two, 436 yards. The railway runs in full view, psychologically looming large along the right side of the fairway. The left side is packed with bunkers, tightening the driving area. The day before Ballesteros had struck a 'safe' 1-iron out to the right and when it finished unplayably behind a concrete out-of-bounds post he scored a 6, his only double-bogie in the championship. "Seve, don't be stupid this time," the Spaniard said to himself. "Play a 2-iron. Be solid. Concentrate. Hit the ball hard."

Hit hard, the ball was blown safely away from the tracks and finished 288 yards down the fairway. In reply, Irwin took a 3-wood – one of his strongest clubs – lifted his body in his downswing, and 'came off the ball'. It was a dreadful stroke, perhaps only 240 yards long, and came to rest on top of a grassy cross-bunker. The American stared after it in disbelief.

"Bring the bag!" Irwin called moments later from atop the bunker, and drew a 6-iron. His caddy, Ian Conner, thought: that's not enough club. You'll never reach. Conner was right. Irwin's shot bounced in the fairway and pulled up some twenty yards short of the green. He marched after it and when he got to its pitch-mark he took an exaggerated pace to the ball, demonstrating to the gallery that it

had rolled only a yard. The American's concentration clearly had departed and, attempting to pitch-and-run his ball, he knocked it through the green. Irwin was beginning to disintegrate. Referee Behrend felt both a pang of unease and pity: bad luck, he thought: you struck the ball well.

Ballesteros's concentration, unlike the American's, was full. Having neatly wedged to twenty-five feet, he lined up his putt. It was uphill, breaking left to right. He thought: be very careful, the green is fast and the wind is behind you. Try only to stroke the ball close to the hole. Don't stand long over it; you'll lose your balance. He hit his ball smartly. It rolled close to the hole for his par. Irwin took three putts and, with a 6, lost the lead for good to the Spaniard.

Walking towards the third tee, Irwin

Hale Irwin, who by the thirteenth fairway, on the last day, appeared to have abandoned hope of victory. As Dick Taylor put it in the American magazine *Golf World*, he "kept his hands in his pockets as if avoiding the check."

cursed loudly and beat his driver on the ground. Conner attempted to calm him. "That's your first 6," he said. Irwin corrected him. "No, it isn't. I had two yesterday." Ballesteros heard the discussion and felt in command.

Third hole, 458 yards. The best line to the green is less perilously close to the railway than it is on the second and, after unloading a huge 2-iron that cleared the corner of a bunker 256 yards down the left, the Spaniard was left with a 9-iron pitch for his par 4. He got it; so did Irwin. "We will forget about Irwin," the Spaniard nevertheless told his caddy. "Other players are coming into the game."

By the time Ballesteros reached the sixth tee, after he and Irwin each had bogied the fourth and parred the fifth holes, other players had indeed come into the game.

Roger Davies, the Australian in his signature plus-fours, and Ben Crenshaw, the best American player never to have won a major title, had both scored three straight birdies through the seventh (or 61st) hole, were in the lead, one stroke under par for the championship. Ballesteros was level. Irwin was one over, Nicklaus and James two over and the Japanese Isao Aoki, making waves up ahead, was on the 8th fairway and also two over par.

The chief feature of the sixth hole, 486 yards and par 5, is man-made. It is a huge

---

Glorious Failure: Seve blasts from a bunker on the fourth hole during the last day at Lytham but, after the ball came to rest four feet from the flag, he missed the putt for a par. It was to be the only time the Spaniard failed to 'get up and down' in two shots from a green-side bunker during the championship.

Trouble. Ballesteros, one of the finest bunker players in the game, explodes from a bunker during the 1979 Masters. So bright is the white sand at Augusta that the following year, when he won the title, the Spaniard wore a peaked cap to protect his eyes against the glare. *Left*: If sand holds no terrors for him, Seve is only human when it comes to water. In the 1979 Ryder Cup matches against the United States at Greenbrier, North Carolina he drops out of a water hazard under penalty.

Victory at Royal Lytham and St. Annes. Ballesteros, together with his playing partner, Hale Irwin, reaches the final green and the moment of triumph in the 1979 Open championship. The win, greeted by wild enthusiasm from the thousands who ringed the green, was the first achieved by a European in the Open since Tony Jacklin won a decade earlier, also at Lytham.

Ballesteros dangles down, head up, from the 'Gravity Gym' he has set up in his new home in Pedrena. The exercising device, which he first saw in 1979 at the home of Graham Marsh, the Australian player, helped ease Seve's back trouble before his victory in the 1980 Masters.

sand hill, which would have stood as one of Lytham's 'terrifying monuments of industry' which Darwin referred to nearly seventy years earlier in his *Great Courses*. The hole had been a flat, weak dog-leg 5 prior to 1965 but one winter night the problem was solved by the R and A's Colin Maclaine, then chairman of the greens committee. He called the local council, and about one thousand tons of sand, blown from the beaches on to the city streets, were dumped across the knee of the dog-leg, 240 yards out from the tee. Gorse and spindly trees soon covered Maclaine's Mound and the hole now offered a temptation: deftly draw a long drive through a prevailing right to left cross-wind over the corner of the mound and you were sitting pretty with a mid-iron shot or less to the green. Fail to clear the mound and descend into purgatory.

Ballesteros so far in the championship had successfully drawn his drive round the mound and three times birdied the hole. This time he let loose with another gigantic drive – and straightaway was in trouble. The ball climbed high over the mound but, in the wind, swung in a huge parabola to the left, to fall out of sight. Irwin watched transfixed, thinking: that could be the wildest drive I've ever seen in a championship. Referee Behrend watched, petrified, thinking: Oh, God, all I need is a lost ball ruling.

The shot was authentically awful. It carried the mound, pitched in the rough, galloped across the adjacent 14th fairway, and finished near the 13th green, again in the rough, ninety yards off line. Later it caused Ballesteros to say, "If Nicklaus had been some of the places I was at Lytham he'd have shot an 80."

Musgrove had never before viewed the 6th green from this vantage – or disadvantage – point in his life. This looks odd, he thought: the gallery standing round the green with their backs to us, not knowing we're coming straight over their heads. Ballesteros's ball was sitting up in an inviting bit of rough. It was a 'flier' lie – one that would not allow him enough clean contact, clubface on ball, to supply spin to 'stop' his shot on the green. "I'll play short," Seve told his caddy. "I'll hit it to the front and right of the green, and chip up." Musgrove nodded, amused. No, you won't play short, he thought. You'll go for the flag. You always do.

Musgrove was right. Ballesteros smashed a high, windblown shot which both he and his caddy lost against the dark clouds. It finished some sixty yards over the green, in rough, and from there the Spaniard, with the touch of a jeweller, got down in 5. A par. Seve was now a stroke behind Davis, level with Crenshaw.

Ballesteros was on track. On the par 5 seventh, 551 yards long but eminently birdie-able in the downwind, Irwin played a glorious second shot, a 5-iron to the unseen heart of the green, but was unmoved by the prolonged cheer rolling back to him. "It won't matter," Irwin said to his caddy, "Ballesteros will get his birdie somehow." His forecast was to be fulfilled: Ballesteros, after an equally sensational second shot, missed an eagle putt from six feet for a birdie. But Irwin, with a chance for *his* eagle and a share of the lead, missed from *four* feet.

Neither Ballesteros nor Irwin made ground on the eighth or ninth holes, and the Spaniard turned in 34 strokes, one under par, while the American was 37. Irwin, putting a forefinger to his temple, figuratively blew out his brains. The scoreboard, with all the leaders heading for home, read: Ballesteros together with Davis (who turned in 32 strokes, and had now played 11 holes) one stroke under par; Crenshaw, after 11 holes, and Irwin, level par; Nicklaus and James, after 10, both −2.

When championships are recalled years after the event it is the spectacular moments, successful and disastrous, which come to mind. But any champion will tell you of other, perhaps single moments when the title nearly slipped away without ceremony. Such was the case of the tenth hole, par 4, at Lytham when Seve nearly lost his way on the final day.

"My confidence was down on this hole," said Ballesteros. "All week I had not once got on the green in two strokes." This time from the fairway, he tried a shot foreign to his nature: a punched 5-iron which, had it come off, would have bored through the wind, checked on the fairway and run into the flag. It didn't come off. The Spaniard pulled the ball, which bounced meekly into the rough, twenty yards to the left and below the level of the green. He was left with a shot of the utmost delicacy: a tiny flip through a cross wind, and yet a shot not hit so strongly as to set the ball rolling down the sloping green and away from the hole. The ideal landing area was four square feet.

The shot failed. The ball fell short and nestled in the long grass, three feet from the green. The job now was to get on to the putting surface, but somehow stop the ball near to the cup: once it slid past Ballesteros would be looking at a calamitous six, two over par. He took a putter from off the green but, so anxious was he not only to run the ball close but to hole it, that he knocked the ball ten feet beyond the cup. "David, maybe we are going to make a double-bogie on this hole," he said to his caddy. "If I miss now, it's all over."

Ballesteros addressed the putt, a greasy side-hiller – a 'knee-knocker', in American parlance – and holed it. He had scored a five on a par 4 hole – as had Irwin – dropped a shot and probably the lead. Yet Ballesteros flung up his arms in relief. "That putt was the most important shot I made all day," he said later. "If I had missed that one I would have lost the championship." He parred 11 and 12.

The thirteenth hole is only 339 yards long and is generally played with a following wind. A punitive ditch trails down the left side of the fairway and both sides are peppered with bunkers, notably a huge one in a sandhill, thirty-eight yards short of the heavily – indeed bafflingly – contoured green. De Vicenzo had advised Ballesteros always to attempt the drive there but, with strange caution, Seve had played it with an iron in the first three rounds.

Victory salute: The Spanish conqueror, his title safe, marches towards the final green on a wave of acclaim – not least from the man with the paddle sign.

On the tee, Ballesteros again reached for an iron. Musgrove said, "Maybe if you hit a drive you can reach the green." Ballesteros often takes advice from de Vicenzo but rarely from his caddy, especially when it is unsolicited, but this time he agreed. How far is the mound? "296 yards," said Musgrove. What did he need to get over the mound? "It's got to be 300 yards to carry." Ballesteros set himself up for a monumental drive down the right side of the fairway – so unexpected an approach that the referee had to stop play to move a photographer out of the way. Ballesteros crashed his drive and, wind-blown, it struck the distant mound two feet below the top and trickled back into the bunker. Give or take an inch, Ballesteros had hit a 298-yard drive *all carry*.

Ballesteros was exactly 68 yards from the flag and faced with one of the most difficult shots in golf: the long fairway bunker shot to the pin. He takes up the story. "I would have tried to play a sand wedge this time but the top of the bunker was too high to get over," he said. "Sometimes it's good to play a pitching wedge in those places, so I hit the ball very hard. But I spin it too much; the ball hits the green, pin high, but it bounces to the right too much, and rolls just off the green." He putted uphill and through a cross-wind, ten yards, and holed it for a birdie. Seve took the lead.

On the fourteenth, Ballesteros made use of the thin rough out to the right which, even after ten years, after reseedings and cartloads of fertilizer, had recovered fully from the trampling it got when that other great European, Jacklin, won the championship. The gusts, now nearly head-on for his second shot, could not foil his splendidly drilled long-iron into the green, but once there Ballesteros was defeated by the wind. It did not, as he had reckoned on, stop his putt from breaking down a slope, and the Spaniard took three putts and a bogie 5. Ballesteros was now level with Crenshaw.

In the view of the master, Jack Nicklaus, there is no tougher championship finish than the last long treacherous four holes at Lytham. At least Ballesteros might have taken comfort, as he stood on the fifteenth tee, for had he not played these holes better than anyone else in the field? It would be remarkable, and perhaps the measure of the champion-to-be, that out of a field of 150 he alone was to play them under par.

It was broken country on the fifteenth freeway, full of unpredictable depressions and clumps of grass, and Ballesteros's drive skipped left into the rough. As Musgrove laboured towards it a BBC television buggy bounced past, its cameramen passing on a message of good news. Davis had crashed, was gone, and Crenshaw had just spent time in the bunker on the 17th, dropping two shots. Ballesteros was two strokes ahead of the field.

The ball was found on clean, matted rough. "Crenshaw took a six at the seventeenth," Musgrove told the arriving Spaniard. Heartened, Ballesteros struck a big 4-iron and broke into a run, eager to hit the ball again. Any single shot from now on may have been the one that won the title, but among them Ballesteros's next must rank high. It was a feathery 35-yard chip, out of short rough and over a bunker, that settled three feet from the flag. Ballesteros holed for his par and checked the scoreboard. He was level after 15, and in a commanding position; Nicklaus and Crenshaw were +2 after 16 and 17 respectively; James and Davis both +3, after 16 and 17, while Irwin had just dropped another shot and fallen to +4.

The next hole, the sixteenth, was to yield up Seve's 'parking lot shot' which was both the most famous and most misunderstood the Spaniard ever hit in his life. It is a seemingly straightforward hole of 353 yards, no challenging distance, especially when you stand on the tee and a smart wind tears at your right hip pocket. The conventional wisdom for the drive was expressed in the championship programme by the canny Maclaine. "The real point about the tee shot is that it has to be farther left than your instinct might decree," wrote the Championship Committee chief.

Y ou're the champion': Irwin congratulates the young conqueror moments before victory.

"The green slopes from right to left."

Ballesteros had early on jettisoned such conventional wisdom. Yes, with the green sloping towards you it would appear best to attack from the left side of the fairway. But in the Spaniard's view that theory was blown out of the window by the prevailing wind which, flush at your back from that left entry point, was strong enough to wreak havoc on any attempt to stop a chip shot on the green.

Ballesteros concluded that the best entry on to the green under these last-round circumstances was from the right. He also considered that any drive that wandered off the fairway to the right would fetch up in harmless rough. Again, he had one of his bare patches in mind. Finally, as he stood on the tee that last time he looked some thirty yards beyond his safe patch of rough. Cars were parked in rows – an overspill from nearby parking area. The cars, he recognised, were an added attraction; for Rule 31 of the rules of Golf declares, "A player may obtain relief from interference by an immovable obstruction without penalty . . ."

So he duly and intentionally drove there. It was a powerful, pumped-up drive which was later to measure 286 yards, and wide of the fairway by 24 yards. "I tell you, I wasn't worried," Ballesteros said later. "The drive wasn't wild, like everybody thought."

As he moved down the fairway, he seemed composed. His two brothers, Vicente and Baldomero, circled around, exhorting him in Spanish, "Don't worry, don't worry! You are two strokes in front." Ballesteros's composure departed briefly as he reached the crowd gathered quiet as though at a road side accident. Where was the ball? he demanded of his caddy. Musgrove shot back: "I don't know. Under there somewhere."

It was indeed under a car, and Referee Behrend, relieved that his first crisis was easily solved, made clear the ruling: Ballesteros could drop free of the obstruction. He did so and, standing quietly, considered the shot. He decided to pace off the distance to the green himself – 64 yards – and pressed the putting surface with his spikes, feeling its firmness. He detected a faint sponginess in a

circle of about 20 feet in diameter and some fifteen feet to the right and past the flag. This and not the flag itself would be his target.

"Play to that spot and make a four," he told himself, back at his ball, worming his feet into the rough. "Play it a little bit left, into the cross wind." The shot, a sand-wedge, was perfect. It floated down into the dead centre of Seve's target, bounced twice and came to rest twenty feet past the pin.

And that was his 'parking lot' shot. That Ballesteros holed the uphill putt into the wind for a birdie has been all but forgotten.

Walking to the seventeenth tee, which faced into the wind, he asked for a 'windie', that is, a ball with smaller dimples which stays 'under the wind' and therefore flies farther. "What number?" asked Musgrove. Seve, recognising the moment said: "Number One."

After the seventeenth, where he had to save par from a bunker, Ballesteros at last arrived on the final tee of the championship. The eighteenth is not a long hole, only 386 yards, yet it is hazardous: gorse bushes to the right, deep rough to the left and dead ahead, immeasurably worse, clusters of bunkers set diagonally across the fairway at driving length. The landing area between these bunkers covers about thirty-five square yards. "Not much of a target for a driver," wrote Pat Ward-Thomas of the London *Guardian*, "when the ambition of a lifetime is within sight."

Ballesteros entertained his own thoughts. On practice days he had studied both the fairway and the rough. His strategy was clear. "Don't put the ball on the fairway because it may roll into a bunker," he told himself. "Aim straight at the rough. It's okay." He chose to play a 3-wood, reasoning, "In case I cut the ball, it will stop quick on the fairway."

Once again there was method in his madness. He smashed a towering tee shot, straight left into the sky. It dropped out of

S eve and brother Baldomero, shortly after the young Spaniard holed out on the final green at the 1980 Open championship.

sight. "What's over there?" shouted Ballesteros, suddenly alarmed, and the cheeky Musgrove replied, "I don't know, that's about the one place we haven't been this week."

As Ballesteros made his way towards his ball he pondered aloud: "We can win with a five."

Musgrove shot back, "We can win with a six. But we need a four. I've got a £1 bet with Barnesy's caddy that somebody finishes under par for the championship."

"Okay, Davy. I will get you your four."

The ball lay on trodden rough. In normal times the shot to the green would call for a 4-iron, but Ballesteros was mindful not only of his pumping adrenalin but of the flower beds lying against the clubhouse through the green. He selected a 5-iron, played it firmly, finishing upright, and the ball danced down the fairway, on and on, finishing at the front of the green. The crowd surged in across the fairway, restrained by stumbling policemen. On the other side of the fairway Irwin and his caddy were engulfed in a stampede. The American, buffeted, raised his sand-wedge and, using it as a weapon, beat his way through the mob. "That crowd went absolutely crazy," he later recalled. "I've been angry and upset on a golf course before, but I've never been truly frightened. It was an ugly scene."

Irwin drew out a white handkerchief and waved it. It was seen by the crowd as a gesture of surrender to Ballesteros. "It wasn't," he

A ny Questions? George Simms, press tent supremo, beckons to a member of the world's press following Seve's victory.

The 1980 Championship trophy, held high by Seve and his brothers (*from left*), Baldomero, jr., Manuel and Vincente in front of the clubhouse at Lytham.

later explained. "It was a gesture of surrender to the mob. I'd been fighting myself for seventeen holes and I didn't need to fight these people."

Irwin is an honourable loser, however, and moments later, after he had dutifully putted out of turn to allow the last putt to the champion, he walked over to Ballesteros. "Before you hole this putt, Seve," he said, "I want to tell you what a great player you are. And a great champion. Congratulations."

The Spaniard nodded his appreciation and, with two putts for the title, he holed the first. As he raised his arms in triumph, children burst on to the green to acclaim their young hero. Several asked if they might keep the ball as a souvenir. Ballesteros accepted their congratulations, but no, the ball was not for them. It was for Señor Santiuste, his first benefactor; his friend from Pedreña.

Putting I: Over the Ball

By now in our instructions, we should have reached the green and, certainly in scoring terms, the most important part of the game. I have already discussed my style of putter, the ping-type. Now the grip. I use the reverse overlap, with the fingers of the right hand down the shaft. I think it is easier to hold the club lightly in this way and, very important, it helps you to distribute evenly the pressure from both hands on the club.

Stance: If you ask me about this, I must think a minute since, for me, the stance is not too important because, as I have said about other shots, comfort is the crucial key to a good golf shot. My stance changes a little from year to year – because of comfort. Basically, though, I think your feet should be a little closer together than the width of your shoulders. A little open? A little closed? It doesn't matter much.

In ball placement, my rules are orthodox: when, in the past I putted with a fairly square stance, I played the ball opposite my left toe; but now, as this book is written, I'm a little open, with the ball nearer to being opposite my left heel.

Stroke: My putting stroke is different from most players. My eyes are above the ball and I am concentrating on it, straight down the shaft, as most players do. But, I *am not* looking only at the ball. Out of the bottoms of my eyes I'm also looking at the heel of my putter. In this way, I can keep the heel of my blade square to the ball. Another player I have noticed doing this is one of the finest putters in the world, the Japanese player, Isao Aoki. Anyway, as a boy, I used to practise this by sticking a thin piece of white tape on the heel of my putter so it would catch my eye. Then, as I brought the putter back, I could keep it square. This idea of looking at the ball and the heel of the club – or maybe the toe, instead, if you like – at the same time will work for

shortish putts, say, up to ten feet. In putts longer than that, the clubhead moves too far to watch it in this way.

Striking the ball: I strike the putt differently than most other players, too. I always either hook or cut the ball on impact – unless the putt is very short. If the borrow is from right to left, I try to hook the ball because the more you hook it the more it spins towards the hole. In the same way, if the break is left to right, I cut the ball to take advantage of the slope. Scientists say that after a few inches such sidespin has no important effect on the path the ball takes but I don't believe them. Besides, such 'hooking' and 'slicing' improves my 'feel'.

The Pendulum: Finally, the most important thing in putting is keeping a pendulum swing. Make your swing move the same distance, at the same speed and height, backwards and forwards – like the pendulum of a clock. To get good pendulum rhythm, practise distance putting with several balls. Keep your feet in place and drag each ball in front of you, then putt it – one-two-one-two-one-two – in rhythm. Forget about the hole and in this way you will not interrupt your rhythm by taking aim at it. You are practising distance and learning rhythm, nothing else. Another exercise, which I mentioned earlier, is to practise putting in the evening darkness – that way you *can't* look at the hole.

Distance putting: I think it should be worked on. I think distance putting is my strong point, and this is good for my confidence, and it will be for yours. I think I have had very few 3-putt greens in my career. I remember in 1977 I played fourteen straight tournament rounds without a single 3-putt green. I think we both would settle for that throughout our playing days.

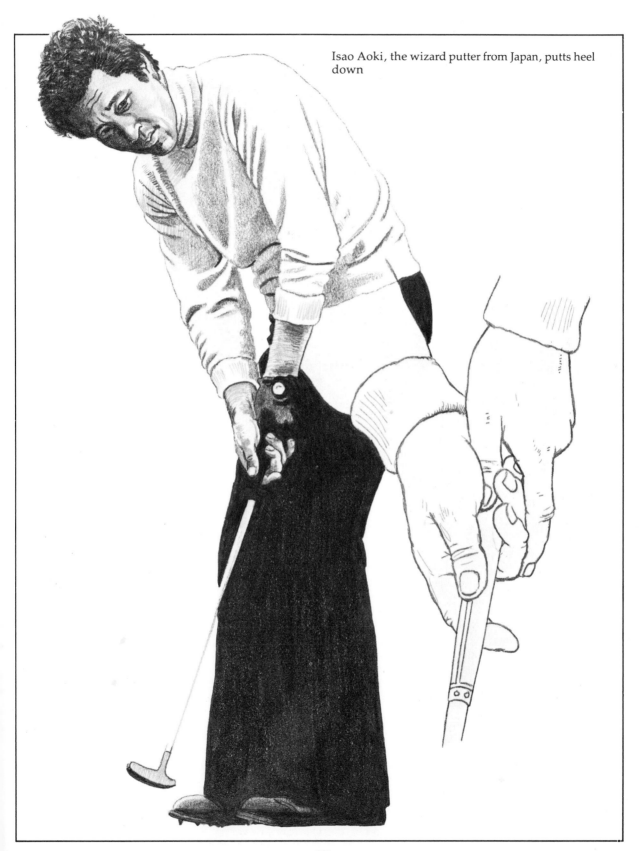

Isao Aoki, the wizard putter from Japan, putts heel down

CHAPTER SIX

TO THE MARKETPLACE

"Seve, unless his putting stroke deserts him, should become the richest Spaniard since Queen Isabella."

Jim Murray, sports columnist,
Los Angeles Times, in 1976

S-e-v-e-r-i-a-n-o B-a-l-l-e-s-t-e-r-o-s: the name, counted out to twenty characters, made up probably the longest in sport. And, thought Ed Barner, Seve's American manager, one of the most unpronounceable. How could you get all those letters on the head of a golf club? Or a television commentator get his tongue round such a mouthful?

"What's your nickname?" asked Barner. "What do they call you at home?"

"Seve." He pronounced it in the Spanish manner: Sebbay.

"What's your mother's maiden name?"

"Sota."

"Don't the Spanish usually use their mother's maiden name as a last name?" asked Barner. "What do you think about using 'Seve Sota'?"

The Ballesteros brothers, Severiano and Manuel, turned mutinous. They were willing to take on Seve's nickname, but there was no way Severiano was going to relinquish his father's family name, and together they said as much. Barner dropped the surname issue and that evening, 19 October 1975, in a hotel room near Orlando, Florida, a star was launched: Seve Ballesteros.

That settled, Barner then turned to some home truths. He had been disappointed by the boys showing up late for their appointment in his hotel suite. The Spaniards had dined with Orville Moody, the 1969 US Open champion. Moody, a Barner client, had gone through some lean years since this success and further embittered by an early experience of bad agenting, had planted doubts about managers in the boys' minds. Barner therefore made one point clear: he could not make money for Ballesteros until the young Spaniard had shown he was a winner.

At the time Ballesteros was all but unknown in America, never having played there, and very much unproven in his native Europe. In the 1975 season, his second on the British PGA tour, he was ranked just 26th on the Order of Merit and was still to win a tour tournament. Barner, acting on the advice of de Vicenzo and Billy Casper, recognised that golf was looking for just such an exotic young player.

"Seve was one of the best-looking young men in sport," he recalled later. "He didn't fall into the blonde-and-boring category of young Americans all trying to look like Johnny Miller."

At that point Barner's stable of golfers, while small, ranged from the great through the insignificant to the hardy perennial. They numbered Johnny Miller, Billy Casper, Lou Graham (who that summer had won the US Open championship at Medinah), Jerry Heard, Dave Hill, John Schroeder (son of the legendary tennis player, Ted Shroeder), J.C. Snead and J.C.'s evergreen uncle, Sam Snead. As Chief Executive Officer of Uni-Managers International (UMI), with offices in Los Angeles, London, Melbourne and Osaka, Barner believed he was not their 'agent' so much as their manager. "An agent is a flesh-peddler, a seller of the body," he says. "We are managers. A manager is concerned with career development, career direction, the well-being of his client."

That he knows little about golf means not a whit to Barner. "I don't know anything about singing either, yet I've represented singers," he says. "The trouble with sports managers in the past is that they've been too enamoured of the game to get down to business."

The career of Edward Lee Barner, so deeply entwined with Ballesteros's, is a remarkable story in itself. Born 10 May 1940 in Arizona, son of a car mechanic, he set his eyes on a career in television production. "I wasn't interested in games as a boy," he recalls. "And I've never played a sport in my life." He earned a degree in Communications and Public Relations from Brigham Young University in Utah and, fulfilling his obligations as a Mormon, a religion descending from his mother, he served thirty months as a missionary in West Berlin.

He then returned to the United States where he worked as a radio and television broadcaster in California, Texas and Utah before, at the age of 25, he became a tour manager for a firm of Hollywood show business agents, Durgom-Katz Associates. "I did everything from hiring musicians to arranging costumes to picking up fifty Grand and banking it."

He travelled with the pop singer, Trini Lopez, and at one time was assigned to London where the motion picture *The Dirty Dozen* was on location. It starred three of the agency's top actors, Telly Savalas, Charles Bronson and Lee Marvin. "One of my jobs," he recalls with a wry smile, "was to hold their hands and keep them out of trouble."

However, the occasional excitements of working with film stars held little attraction for Barner, and in 1967 he left the agency, anxious, as he says, to work in a field where excellence alone was rewarded. "In entertainment," he argues, "talent has very little bearing on success, whereas in sports, regardless of how you look or talk, if you can do it you can be Number One."

The bridge to sports management came through Barner's Mormon connections, for at that time the Mormons had very much a Number One star – golfer Billy Casper. Casper had once been a client of the dominant Mark McCormack, the established sportsmen's manager who looked after the affairs of golf's Big Four, Arnold Palmer, Jack Nicklaus, Gary Player and Casper himself. He had left McCormack, however, because he felt too much attention was being given to Player and even more to Palmer. For example, he felt aggrieved over a slacks contract that went to Palmer in 1959. Casper had won the US Open championship that summer. McCormack had approached a slacks manufacturer with a view to an endorsement contract but the manufacturers, unenthusiastic about dressing the rotund Casper, went for Palmer instead.

Thus Casper left McCormack and took on another manager, Wally Dill. He began to slim. He was playing in the 1967 Sahara Classic in Las Vegas at the same time that Trini Lopez was in town. Barner, who shortly was to quit his agency job, had read about Casper, a fellow churchman and Californian: he sent him a 100-pound basket of organically-grown fruit together with an invitation to dinner. Casper accepted, and the following year they formed their firm, Uni-Managers International (UMI).

In 1969 the new firm took aboard their first major client, their fellow Mormon John Miller, who, as a 19-year-old Brigham Young university student, had electrified golf by finishing eighth to Casper in the 1966 US Open in Miller's native San Francisco. Barner knew his show-business and one of his first moves was to alter Miller's name. Forthwith he was not to be 'John' but 'Johnny' Miller. "'John' is a cold name, anonymous like 'John Doe'," Barner explains. "'Johnny' has a homey, American ring – you know, like 'Johnny Comes Marching Home Again' and Johnny Appleseed [of American legend fame]. It made him sound more approachable. Honestly, calling him 'Johnny' had a great deal to do with his commercial success."

Miller, as Ballesteros was to do later, resisted such a change. But unlike Ballesteros

Miller found an avenue of compromise. To make his point and keep his independence he signed autographs 'John ny' for years afterwards, leaving a gap between the 'n's. Miller became a small shareholder in UMI, a position he retained until the expiration of the Barner-Miller contract in 1979, and according to Barner, earned in excess of $10 million over the decade of their association. His endorsements were wide-ranging, from razor blades to hotels, and included most famously the $1 million contracts to model an inexpensive line of clothes by Sears.

That the breadth of Miller's earnings were so remarkable has most to do with his tournament successes, likeability and good looks. Unlike Arnold Palmer, golf's trailblazing multi-millionaire, Miller is no workaholic. More at ease chopping wood at home than posing in front of advertisers' cameras in Acapulco, he had to be pushed. Barner pushed him and found a way through Miller's nonchalance. It was an illuminating and profitable experience for both men. On Miller – and for Miller – Barner cut his big-time teeth.

To understand what Seve was to experience, and suffer, it is important first to understand the world of commerce that had grown up round his sport. In fact, great golfers through history have traded on their names. The ball and clubmakers Willie Park and old Tom Morris, winners of the initial Open championships (then called The Belt) of 1860 and 1861, were early examples. Morris literally posted the dates of his championship triumphs and those of his son Young Tom – eight in all – outside their shop in St. Andrews. And Park's son, Willie Junior, was no doubt helped in his career as a golf course architect by his own championship victory in 1887.

The early clubmaker champions stamped their names on their handmade clubs, of course; but it wasn't until before the First War that a champion sold his signature to a clubmaker other than one to whom he was attached. He was James Braid, one of the famous Triumvirate with J. H. Taylor and Harry Vardon, who among them won eight Opens in the first decade of this century. Braid, who had made clubs for the Army and Navy Stores, struck a bargain with William Gibson and Company, clubmakers, of Kinghorn, Fifeshire – a 6p royalty for each club in a 7-club set of irons.

The game, meanwhile, was enjoying its first 'explosion'. This was touched off by another member of the Triumvirate, Harry Vardon, the finest player of his day, who fanned interest in the game through an exhibition tour of America. The tour was sponsored by the American ballmakers, A. J. Spalding Brothers, and during it Vardon played Spalding's gutta percha (Malaysian rubber) ball called the Vardon Flyer. Sponsorship on a big scale had begun.

After the War the exhibition tour was brought to a fine, flamboyant art form by the American Walter Hagen. Hagen, dapper and stylish, travelled the world, gliding up to clubhouses in chauffeur-driven Rolls-Royces, dancing the night away at extravagant parties at such grand hotels as London's Savoy. "I never wanted to be a millionaire," he said. "I just wanted to live like one."

Hagen won the American Open in 1914 and 1919 and became the first American to dominate the Open, winning the British title in 1922, 1924, 1928 and 1929. Along the way he expanded the exhibition into the great 72-hole challenge match, once, in 1926, drubbing Bobby Jones 11 and 10 to collect $6,800. He was the resourceful promoter of equipment, too: for $1,500, for example, he promoted the first tee peg, invented by a New Jersey dentist, cunningly leaving the wooden mementoes to be scrambled for as he marched off the tee.

His most splendid coup, worthy of an Ed Barner or a Mark McCormack, was to carry 22 clubs in his bag – more than fourteen clubs in a bag was legal in those days – because a golf club manufacturer had agreed to pay him $500 for each of his clubs the great man carried. In retirement Hagen lent his name to the Wilson Sporting Goods Company as head of the 'Hagen Equipment Division'. As for the breadth of his fortune, Hagen once spoke of making $22,000 and losing $20,000 in a year:

by this measurement he never was a million-aire.

Ironically, the finest golfer to earn $1 million from the game was the greatest amateur of them all: Bobby Jones. As Jones's popularity soared through the late 1920s he wrote a syndicated column for the North American Newspaper Alliance, an arrangement which at the time did not violate his amateur status.* Then, upon his retirement after winning the 1930 Grand Slam (the Amateur and Open titles in both Britain and America), Jones set about designing one of the first matched sets of clubs which, under his signature, were marketed by A. J. Spalding in 1932.

There also were books by Jones, chiefly the classic *Down the Fairway* and, most profitable of all, a series of eighteen short films. These films, twelve in a series called *How I Play Golf* and six more called *How to Break 90*, ran only fifteen minutes each but, sparkling with ad-libbed plots and a cast of characters which included W. C. Fields, Douglas Fairbanks Jr., Joan Blondell and James Cagney, were runaway successes at the movie houses of America. Such a folk hero was Jones that Warner Brothers paid him an estimated $250,000 for his part in the films, an astonishing sum for the Depression years.

Meanwhile, on the other side of the Atlantic Henry Cotton was emerging as the greatest British player between Vardon and Jacklin. Open winner three times (1934, 1937 and 1948), he too brought his talents to the market-place through endorsements and

exhibitions. In later life he turned to golf course architecture, and developed the Penina Golf Hotel and course in the Algarve, Portugal.

"He is one of the most aggressive businessmen in world golf," the respected American golf writer, Bob Harlow claimed in a 1951 magazine article. Oddly, however, Cotton was exploited. His most famous deed on a golf course, his marvellous score of 65, returned in the second round and *en route* to his 1934 Open victory at Royal St. George's, Sandwich, earned him hardly a pittance. Three years later, in honour of this score, Dunlop, as part of their golf range, launched a Dunlop '65' ball. Apart from the war years, it has remained on the market ever since. Cotton was paid nothing for this celebration of his achievement and thereafter received only £150 a year to play it exclusively in tournaments.

At this point along came Samuel Jackson Snead, the self-professed hillbilly, and in tow the game's first agent. Snead turned professional in 1933, the year Jones's new clubs were sweeping the country, and by 1937, the year he won four US tour tournaments, he became a man in demand. It was the urbane, rotund Fred Corcoran, at the time tournament director of the US Professional Golfers' Association, who took him on. Corcoran set up exhibition tours and stunt shows for the irrepressible Snead and once, so the story goes, goaded Snead into playing barefooted on the hallowed turf of Augusta National during the Masters. Corcoran's caper put Snead in the limelight and, thirty years on, 'Slammin' Sam' was still taking curtain calls – only under the management of Ed Barner.

Snead's rival through the 1940s and 50s was Ben Hogan, 'The Wee Iceman', the finest player between the reigns of Jones and Nicklaus. A Texan, Hogan was tough, suspicious, aloof and sometimes downright cold. "Hogan was not the least bit reluctant in pushing the price to the limit the market would bear," Gene Gregston writes in his book, *Hogan, the Man Who Played for Glory*. "He always said no to the first offer, and he was often uncompromising, unyielding and

---

*One's 'amateur status' was as touchy a matter then as it is today. In a celebrated law case, which finally reached the House of Lords, the amateur champion Cyril Tolley successfully sued J. S. Fry and Sons, the chocolate firm, for unauthorised use of a caricature of himself and his caddy to promote a chocolate bar. The caricature "depicted him as playing golf, with a packet of their chocolate protruding from his pocket, and a caddy was represented with him, who also had a packet of chocolate, the excellence of which he likened to the excellence of the plaintiff's drive," read the 1931 law report. ". . . At the trial evidence was given by golfers to the effect that if an amateur golfer lent himself to such a scheme for advertising, people might think he was not maintaining his amateur status, and that he might be called upon to resign his membership in any reputable club." See headnote, Tolley v. J. S. Fry & Sons, Limited [1931] AC 33A.

uncooperative." He would demand money to appear on television news programmes and reportedly earned the princely sum of $5,000 to appear in tournaments.

"I've been criticised for not playing in this tournament or that, or for demanding appearance money or guarantees, by the same fellows [other touring pros] I'm helping," Gregston quotes Hogan as saying. "They don't realize that every time I raise my exhibition fee or the amount of appearance money it's helping all professional golfers. An exhibition fee of $1,000 was unheard of until I got it. But you'll notice when I raise mine others do the same, and the young fellows coming up in the future will be able to demand more because we've raised the level."

One 'young fellow coming up' was Arnold Palmer. Palmer turned professional in 1954 and over the next quarter century transformed the financial face of golf beyond all recognition. He did it through his magnetic personality, dashing style of play and, most importantly, the shrewd management of Mark McCormack, an American lawyer who, as a fine player himself, knew the game intimately.

If Corcoran was the first golfers' manager it was McCormack who realized all that the job might encompass. He had played in a university golf team against Palmer in the early 1950s but it was not until 1958 that they met formally. By then McCormack was a Cleveland attorney, dealing with contracts and general corporate matters and spreading his wings into a company called National Sports Management. In the latter capacity he was booking exhibitions for top American professionals. Palmer that year had won the Masters and through 1959 McCormack booked Palmer for exhibition fees ranging from $350 to $500.

The crucial moment came, as McCormack recounts in his book, *Arnold Palmer, The Man and the Legend*, later that year. Palmer approached McCormack and asked him to explore the vast financial opportunities that were opening before him. "You can work for one or two other golfers later, if you want," Palmer said. "But right now I want you to

Enemy Agent: Mark McCormack, the American business manager who had his eyes on taking over the business interests of the Spaniard.

handle my problems and see what you can do with them." McCormack uneasily accepted the challenge and, as he is fond of saying, a handshake sealed their contract.

McCormack soon saw that the first major job was not to secure new contracts for his client but to break an old one. Wilson Sporting Goods Company, the biggest of its kind in the world, held Palmer in a hammerlock grip. The company not only restricted his opportunities round the world but, as McCormack recounts, even muscled in on other companies' promotions. Wilson had to be mentioned in any other endorsement. "I start off every morning, folks, with a hearty bowl of Crunchy Corn Crackles," joked McCormack. "And my trusty Wilson wedge." Wilson's grasp on Palmer, what is more, kept his earnings from the company to a trickle. In nine years, McCormack estimated, Wilson paid Palmer about $75,000 for ball and club endorsements, a meagre sum considering that by the end of that period he was the holder of four major titles. Palmer and McCormack attempted to buy out their contract but Wilson made them see it through until 1963. Palmer, at last free of his Wilson ties, then started the Arnold Palmer Golf Club Company.

In other areas McCormack was more successful. In a Munsingwear shirt contract, for example, Palmer stood to earn $250 for each nationwide television appearance, a small fee perhaps – until McCormack realised that Palmer had clearly been wearing discernible Munsingwear shirts in thirty-four different nationally-televised cigarette ads: he applied for, and got, a further $8,500.

Palmer's empire now embraces everything from golf equipment to sportswear, insurance, publishing and motels. "You can shave with his lather, spray on his deodorant, drink his favourite soft drink," writes McCormack. "Fly his preferred airline, buy his approved corporate jet, eat his candy bars, order your stock certificates through him and cut up with his power tools."

As Palmer's empire expanded a proliferation of golfing agents appeared on the American scene: Bucky Woy (Lee Trevino), Dan Murphy (John Mahaffey), Vinnie Giles (Jerry Pate at the time) and Putnam Pierman, an Ohio lawyer, who for a spell took over Nicklaus who, like Casper, felt McCormack was favouring Palmer with his time. However, the new managers slowly faded away, Trevino, Nicklaus, Tom Watson and, to a lesser extent, Miller mostly taking over their own corporate affairs.

Barner's initial contract for Ballesteros, signed only a few weeks after their meeting in Orlando, Florida, was modest: $5,000 a year to use a Japanese club, Mizuno, while in Japan. But in the summer of 1976, the Spaniard hit the world headlines by leading the Open championship for three rounds at Royal Birkdale. That he slipped to second place behind Miller on the last day hardly reduced his appeal: the young Spaniard was an overnight celebrity, and Barner was immediately able to play a 'different ball game', at times literally. "I thought Barner and I had agreed on terms of a new ball contract the day before the Open," recalls Richard Brown of Dunlop Sports Company, Ltd. (UK). "The day after it he made totally new demands."

Barner's version of this encounter is different. "No agreement was made," he says emphatically. "Brown presented a programme which we declined – our listening to his terms did not constitute our agreement."

Dunlop did not meet those demands and since then Barner and Brown have continued to keep their distance. The previous year, 1975, Seve had played in the esteemed Dunlop Masters championship in England but, following the Birkdale disagreement, he only once played in the Dunlop Masters – in

---

Logos: some of the names and trademarks of Seve's worldwide business interests from Braun, the German firm (*upper right*) to the Severiano Ballesteros Golf Club in Japan.

1979, when he needed Order of Merit points. In 1976 he was released to play in the Donald Swaelens Memorial Tournament in Belgium, in 1977 he elected to play an exhibition match in South Africa, and in 1978 he withdrew at the last moment with "a chest infection, exhaustion and a recurrence of his old back injury," according to UMI's official explanation at the time. Ballesteros, it should be noted, was not offered appearance money by Dunlop. In following years it was taken for granted that the Spaniard would not play in the event and, not surprisingly, Brown and Dunlop led the fight against the Spaniard in the acrimonious 'appearance money' battle during the 1981 season.

In 1976, Ballesteros led the British PGA's Order of Merit, and the following year became the hottest property in world golf, winning seven times in six different countries, including Britain and the United States. On the way he became the subject of a bitter take-over battle: McCormack against Barner. In effect, the Spaniard became the central figure in McCormack's plan to dominate and control tournament golf on the Continent. How he was put into such a position was revealed in the spring of 1978 in the London *Sunday Times*.

McCormack, through his firm, International Management Group, was already deeply involved in European golf. He was not only a player's manager but a television commentator (BBC), a magazine publisher (of the now defunct *Golf International)*, a film-maker (the Open, the then Piccadilly World Matchplay championship and a seasonal compendium of the British tour) and much involved in the organization and promotion of major Continental tournaments.

In tandem with Management Européen of Paris, his partners on the Continent, McCormack's plans in Europe for 1978 were stupendous. They were to run the Portuguese, Italian, Swiss, German and Belgium Opens as well as the Laurent Perrier trophy and the Lancome trophy. In Britain they were to organise the Hennessy (European team) Cup, the Colgate Match-play and the British Tournament Players' Division championship.

All in all, McCormack controlled about a third of the entire tour.

Enter Ballesteros, managed by Barner. McCormack was doubly annoyed that not only was the young Spaniard worth a fortune in endorsements and appearance money but the very European tournament sponsors for whom McCormack worked would be willing, indeed eager, to pay appearance fees to his chief rival. Moreover, it would be McCormack's own office who would pay out the money.

Clearly McCormack needed Ballesteros in his camp. To this end on 10 and 11 October 1977 he met with a dozen members of his team in London. The minutes of the meeting were later given to *the Sunday Times*. They read, in part:

"It seems that Ballesteros is unhappy with Barner, and now may be the time to approach him. The stronger we become in golf, the more Barner is able to do for Balle-

Cover boy: Seve, by the time he was 20, was a regular face on the front of magazines around the world.

steros, so it is important to have Ballesteros. It was [*sic*] felt that an investment in hiring the person closest to Ballesteros to work for us in Spain [e.g. Manuel Ballesteros or (Jorge) Ceballos (chief executive of the Spanish PGA)] should be considered if this would guarantee us Severiano Ballesteros as a client. At present, Ceballos is an obstacle in our way. He certainly has a big influence on [Spanish player Antonio] Garrido and we think he is trying hard to influence Ballesteros as well.''

The approaches to the Spaniards came to nothing. For himself, Seve at that point in his career wanted little more in life than to hit a golf ball, crooked or straight, and he stayed loyal to Barner.

In March 1978 Barner met in Paris with officials of Management Européen; later a letter was delivered to him by hand. It spelled out appearance fees that would be offered to Ballesteros: Portuguese and French Opens, $3,000; Belgian, German, Swiss, Moroccan, Laurent Perrier and Hennessy events, $4,000 each; Lancome Trophy and Italian Open, $5,000 each and Barcelona Cup, $7,500. The total, $47,500, was an astonishing figure at the time. (It would double and redouble and three years later break the bank.) No one in European golf history, not even Jacklin under McCormack, had commanded such fees. In fact, Peter Oosterhuis, Ballesteros's immediate predecessor as Europe's leading player, earned less than that ($17,454) when he led the money-winners in 1973.

The offer continued: ''Moreover, we will pay for air fare tickets, to and from Spain, and also pay hotels and meals for two, including Manuel. On the other hand Seve will not play in either the Scandinavian Enterprises Open in Sweden or the Dutch Open.'' Golf Européen plainly aimed to weaken these two tournaments which had successfully resisted overtures to be run by their organisation. ''In these conditions we will give to him a bonus of $500 for each tournament victory on the European circuit and, if he is the first on the Order of Merit after the Swiss Open and he plays the Lancome, we will give an additional $5,000 . . . We hope that all these conditions will be agreed to and we will develop our business relations with Seve and UMI.'' The letter was signed by Dominique Molte of Management Européen.

Again the McCormack thinking was clear. If Seve played in the Lancome he could not play in the European Open which was to be played in the same week in England. The European Open was being run by Sven Tumba, the Swede who ran the Scandinavian Enterprises Open which had spurned McCormack. Furthermore, it was being run in partnership with Leisuresports, a group of experienced London sports consultants who at the time were linked with Barner. Finally, the chairman of the European Open advisory board was Nicklaus, who years earlier had split with McCormack. The complex offer, Barner realised, could boost Ballesteros's non-prize money earnings well over $50,000 in Europe alone that summer; but Barner turned it down. ''We're not drawing up a schedule based on politics,'' he said loftily. As it turned out Barner negotiated separate appearance fees for the tournaments, resulting in handsome increases from the original offers. Ballesteros did not play in the Portuguese or Italian championships. One consequence was clear: the battle for Ballesteros was hotting up.

Meanwhile, Ballesteros kept getting richer. By this time Barner had set up the structure of the Spaniard's business. He had also taken on a gifted lawyer and linguist, Joe Collet, a fellow-Mormon fluent in Spanish, Portuguese, German and English. Collet is Executive Vice-President of UMI but his duties almost exclusively lie with his star client. It is Collet who leads the Spaniard through the multi-lingual minefields of contracts and commercial requests, and he who pays the business calls to Pedreña. UMI had become the 'exclusive management representative for Spangoff Enterprises, Inc,' the 'exclusive contracting agent' for Ballesteros. In five years, from that first Japanese club contract in 1976, Ballesteros was led by Barner, through Collet, to some two dozen contracts world wide, from golf equipment to Japanese tomato juice to table-top games. Barner re-

fuses to comment on his clients' incomes, properly enough, but it is understood that they earn him far in excess of $500,000 a year. On average Barner takes about 25 per cent of this net money, an average figure for most sports agents. The Spaniard's earnings, in all, adding prize and appearance money, reach about $1 million a year.

His earning power is becoming realised, more and more, in Spain, a rich market Barner never exploited. The Spanish business, which ranges from soft drinks to 'Seve Tours', that is, packaged tours of Spanish golf complexes, now comes under a separate firm, totally free of UMI. It is called Fairway SA. Its director is Ceballos, who is also an executive of Iberia Airlines and, until he grew tired of charges of favouring Ballesteros, executive director of the Spanish PGA. Fairway was formed in 1981 and expects to turnover $300,000 in 1982. The Ballesteros brothers are the sole shareholders (Seve with 85%, the others with 5% each) and Ceballos, on a modest salary, has no formal contract with the enterprise. He works under a hand-shake, similar to McCormack and Palmer.

While Ballesteros has not made that quantum leap into business wholly unrelated .to golf his portfolio shows a remarkable variety of financial interets, both geographically and in subject matter. For example, he uses different clubs in different countries: in Japan, where he is committed to play in at least two tournaments a year, and the Far East he uses those made by the Mizuno Sporting Goods Company, Ltd., under a contract estimated at $50,000 a year; in the US he swings a Sounder club, and in the United Kingdom and on the Continent Ballesteros plays with Slazenger, at least eight irons in the bag, under a contract that began in the 1981 season and which is worth anything up to £250,000 over five years.

The Slazenger contract, one of his most complex, was of special interest through the 1981 season, the year of the wrangles over appearance money with the European Tournament Players' Division of the British PGA. For a start, the contract carried 'disincentive' clauses; that is Ballesteros was required to play in six British or Continental tour tournaments (not counting the Open) and would suffer reductions in earnings according to how many fewer he played. If he played in none at all he would earn only about forty per cent of the reported £50,000 for the year. What is more, Slazenger also requested the Spaniard to wear shirts with their well-known panther symbol. (In the final round of the 1981 Open at Sandwich Ballesteros had to change into a Slazenger shirt just before his tee-off because he had been seen on the practice ground dressed mistakenly in a shirt meant for wear in Germany.) "These geographically-fragmented contracts can be a pain in the neck," says Ian Peacock, managing director of Slazengers. "We can't use Seve in our international catalogues but, on the other hand, we do pretty well because photographs taken at the Open championship appear round the world with our 'panther' on his shirts."

The most interesting paragraphs of Ballesteros's contract with Slazenger concern the

balls. He is meant to "endeavour to play the Slazenger B51 ball if and when he is satisfied with its performance and quality." The company's research department in Japan (where, ironically, Ballesteros is committed to play the Dunlop ball) has worked mightily on developing a ball that satisfies the Spaniard. They have come up with one that satisfies two of their other players, the Australian Greg Norman and Johnny Miller, and who use it as suggested. Oddly, while satisfied with the new B51, Ballesteros superstitiously keeps to the Acushnet ball, the most popular among professionals, and for which he gets substantial "win bonuses". "He keeps saying he'll get round to the B51 one day," says the good-humoured Peacock, but adds: "he is eroding the credibility of his endorsement."

Contracts come and go, but at one time late in 1981 Ballesteros's other golf or golf-related endorsements included the Dunlop ball in Japan; Dunlop-Slazenger clubs, balls, bags, gloves, shirts and sweaters in Australia; clubs, balls, socks and tee-shirts in Japan; Braun golf clothing in most of Europe; rainwear in the United Kingdom and the United States; Nagura belts and leather-carrying cases in Japan; Segarra Industries Mediterranean golf and casual shoes for the UK and Continental Europe; and columns and instructionals in Britain's *Golf Monthly*, America's *Golf*, and the Scottish *Daily Record*, Scottish *Sunday Mail* and the *Daily Express* in Britain and, more recently, his own table 'golf' game worldwide.

Although Ballesteros still lives in Pedreña, returning there through the year like some lonely homing pigeon, he is 'attached' to two different clubs. In Europe he is the 'touring' professional for La Manga Campo de Golf, on the Costa Blanca in Spain. As part of his arrangement with La Manga his brother Manuel is employed three months a year there as club professional, and when Seve visits the complex he stays in a condominium which one day he will own. In America he is the 'touring' professional for the Doral Hotel and Country Club near Miami, and is identified with the club while playing in the States and Canada. In the Christmas holidays he has in the past spent three days at the club. He gives clinics there and in the February of each year plays in the Doral-Eastern Open, a tournament co-sponsored by the complex, which ties in nicely with his run-up to the US Masters in April. The Doral contract was originally 25,000 dollars a year, but an escalation clause, similar to those found in nearly all his contracts, came into effect with his two major victories: it now approaches 50,000 dollars.

Like many successful players, Ballesteros has also taken a step into the field of golf course architecture. He is Golf Director of The Seve Ballesteros Club, an exclusive golf club complex which is being built near Narita airport, outside Tokyo. He gave advice on the design of the course to the builders, Golf Construction Ltd., a British firm fronted by the television commentator Peter Alliss.

In a publicity stunt at London's Kennington Oval, Ballesteros lofts a ball over mid-off while Surrey's bona-fide cricketer Pat Pocock looks on. They were launching cricket tours to the La Manga Oval, Spain, beginning 1982/3.

The Spaniard wears Rolex watches (for a modest fee, since the two watches he's been given are worth about $6,000 each), and drives a Range Rover whenever he is in Europe (in exchange for three Leyland exhibitions a year). He lends his name to 'Seve Tours', an Iberia Airline promotion to bring foreign golfers to Spain. He appears in five golf clinics, or 'Seve Days', a year at $15,000 a time. In these he gives group instructions, usually to clients of the firm that hires him for the day, and ends each clinic with an exhibition of his remarkable repertoire of trick shots: hitting the ball while standing on one foot, his knees, while blindfold, making balls hook and slice on command. Ballesteros enjoys these days but dreads the cocktail parties and dinners that inevitably follow.

The thrifty Ballesteros spends little of his enormous earnings. They are controlled by his Spanish corporation and are stashed away in banks, mostly in Spain, invested in land and real estate and in blue-chip stock. Barner and his organization do not offer their clients investment advice but encourage a conservative programme. "Seve knows where his money is," says Barner, "and he doesn't want to get rich quick." Want to or not, the Spaniard seems unable to avoid it.

SEVE BALLESTEROS

The champion: this formal photograph, made the morning after a night of celebrating his victory at Augusta, shows Seve in the winner's Green Jacket. Within the week, Ballesteros's managers had run off thousands of glossy promotional reproductions of the photo.

Putting II: Into the Hole

It seems obvious that if you don't aim a putt correctly you will not hole a putt. Yet, the more I play in pro-amateur tournaments, the more I realize that many amateurs don't correctly aim these important shots. They either don't, or they can't, read a green. This is not completely their fault because they play most of the golf on their home courses where they know the greens without thinking about them.

Studying the green: This has been said many times before but it should be said again: study the green. Look at the line of the putt from behind the ball, behind the hole and from either side of the putt. Only in this way can

you see the 'borrow,' as they say in Britain, or the 'break' as they say in America, of the putt. Study which way the grass is lying because, of course, the ball will break left to right, say, if the grass is lying left to right. The ball will travel much faster when the grass lies away from you, slower when it lies towards you. Finally, remember the slower the ball is travelling, the more it will break.

When your putter turns sour: When you are putting badly, don't change your putter, stance or grip while playing. If you change while playing, you will make small changes and probably upset your basic method by taking this compensation. Wait until you are on the putting green where you can rebuild your method from the start.

Remedies: If your bad putting streak goes on for weeks, you need a complete change for your confidence. You must either change the club or the 'feel' of the club by weighting it or building up the grip. Another idea I use is to have two lines scratched across the top of the blade, at the point of ball-impact. This helps me see the line of my stroke. Also, if your bad streak continues, maybe try a darker putter head; a black head provides a contrast with the green of the grass and the white of the ball and the club then feels new and fresh. You will see the putter better and therefore you will get a better sense of direction.

Wet Greens: You obviously strike a ball harder on a wet green but, just as important, when struck harder the ball will tend to hold its line and not break. So you must remember to account for this.

Just off the Greens: Unless the grass is short or the circumstances special, such as a very short putt or lightning-fast green, I rarely use a putter from off the putting surface. Since your ball will be set-up in grass, and your putter has almost no loft, you cannot put any spin on the shot and, therefore, it is almost impossible to control the distance. It is better to chip with a 7-iron, so you can drop the ball where you want and with enough 'stuff' to control the distance.

The Jack Nicklaus Shot: A shot I learned by watching Jack is one that he uses when his ball is sitting deep in the collar of grass round a green. Don't try to chip it clean because you won't be able to judge how well it will come out of the grass. Your club will get snarled in the grass and your ball will do what we call a *salto de rana*, a frog-jump, in Spanish. Instead, take a pitching wedge and strike the ball with the sharp leading edge of the club face, halfway down the ball. It will jump up, get clear of the grass and run into the pin. This shot is valuable but it needs much practice.

And lastly, round the green, I try one hard rule: never leave the ball short of the hole.

The Break: read it from all four quarters

CHAPTER SEVEN

MY COLOUR OF GREEN

"He is something else, this young Spaniard, and all things being equal he has an excellent chance of becoming one of the authentically great golfers of all time."

Herbert Warren Wind, the American golf writer,
in *The New Yorker*, 26 May, 1980

Ballesteros was to travel many times to America before returning with the prize he most coveted – a major US crown, preferably the Masters. The word 'Masters' was in the language of his childhood: it was his window on the outside world. His uncle Ramon Sota played at Augusta six times – first in 1964, finally in 1972 – and tied for sixth place in 1965, the year Seve was 8 and still chipping with stones and, perhaps significantly, the year Nicklaus scored a 271, a Masters' low-scoring record which Seve later would challenge.

The moment he first set foot on the course in 1977, Ballesteros felt at home: the Augusta National Golf Club, while on a grander scale, is similar to the lush, rolling, pine-covered Real Club de Golf de Pedreña. "When I saw it, Augusta gave me a very familiar feeling," Ballesteros recalls. "These were my trees, my colour of green, and I said to myself, 'Seve, one day you will win this tournament.'"

Golf Digest seemed to share this notion in their cover question: "Can This Teen-ager Win the Masters?" The query wasn't altogether fair. Since the Masters was first played in 1934 only two men (Horton Smith in 1934, Gene Sarazen in 1935) had won it first time out and, even more impressively, the youngest player to win the classic event was the greatest golfer ever to play in it, Nicklaus, who captured the title at 23 in 1963. What is more, in 1977 Ballesteros was only lately released from the Spanish Air Force and therefore fairly rusty.

Pointed out as a prodigy, Ballesteros felt under pressure. He nearly succumbed to it for, on the very first day at Augusta, while over-straining to smash a practice ball out of the grounds, he pulled a muscle in his back. He was also suspicious. "The Augusta people are trying to test me," he muttered darkly when he saw he was drawn to play with Nicklaus on the first day. "They want to see how I can take pressure." Ballesteros talked nonsense, for his pairing was meant to be honorific: Europe's best player on display with the world's best.

Ballesteros was introduced on the first tee as the holder of the Dutch Open championship and leader of the British Order of Merit and he stood, eyes down and emotionally impervious. "I was okay until I noticed the sharp contrast between the green grass and the white tee marker," he recalls. "That put a very strange feeling in my stomach. I suddenly realised I was playing in the Masters."

Ballesteros opened the championship uncertainly, with a 74 and 75. As the second evening descended he sat in the players' lounge, watching the last players toiling on television, worrying over missing the midway cut. "Don't worry, you'll make it," I remember telling him. "You're only five strokes over par." The remark angered Ballesteros. "Yes," he snapped, "but if I was five *under* par I would be leading the tournament." He settled down and finished on 291, three over par, fifteen strokes behind the winner, Watson, and joint-33rd. All the same, it was an impressive debut.

Ballesteros's Masters education continued in 1978 when, three under par after three rounds, he played the last day with Gary Player, both lying seven shots behind the leader, Hubert Green. It was to be a memorable day. Player made the turn in 34, useful but nothing spectacular, then scored two more birdies and was only three strokes

adrift of Green as he walked purposefully down the thirteenth fairway with Ballesteros. "Seve, I want to tell you something," he said, and gestured towards the crowd thronging beyond the distant ropes. "Those people don't think I can win. You watch, I'll show them."

He did. In one of the most spectacular finishes in Masters history, Player scored seven birdies over the last ten holes to nip Green, Watson and Rod Funseth by a stroke to win the title. Player's fight, and his remark on the thirteenth fairway, left an indelible impression on the young Spaniard. It reinforced Ballesteros's own siege mentality. "I think Player maybe likes to think people are against him so he can fight harder," Seve said later. "I'm like that. The more against you are the crowd, the more you want to prove something." For himself, Ballesteros's own battle that day brought little reward, a 74 for a shared 17th-place finish.

In 1979, Fuzzy Zoeller won after a playoff with Watson and Ed Sneed. Sneed had let a three-stroke lead slip away over the last three holes, a collapse that would haunt Ballesteros. The Spaniard finished tied for 12th spot, seven behind Zoeller. He felt he could win in 1980.

Accordingly, the Spaniard began to draw up his battle plans. His first rehearsal, with the Masters pointedly in mind, took place in the Suntory World Match-Play championship in the autumn of 1979 on the West Course at Wentworth, near London. Trees crowd the fairways at Wentworth, as they do at Augusta, and in the interest of keeping the ball in play the Spaniard shortened his swing for more control. Ballesteros-watchers could see it clearly: Seve had chopped as much as eighteen inches off the top of his backswing. Under pressure in the championship – Ballesteros lost on the 40th green in the semi-final

_____

round to the Japanese Aoki – he resolutely retained his new, short and serene swing. This act of restraint was one of the most crucial triumphs of his entire career.

Back in Pedreña during the winter he continued his rehearsal, tossing balls willy-nilly into the pine trees and playing out. He drilled himself in big, high shots that curved left, the necessary shape for Augusta, where eleven of the thirteen dog-legs swing in that direction. Yet he was unhappy. His swing had been built partly in the image of Nicklaus's, with a break or 'cock' of the wrists in the takeaway. Ballesteros was finding that this action reduced his control of the club-head, a discovery that Nicklaus had made too. Therefore, in the evenings the Spaniard stood in front of a full-length mirror in the farm-house stables, down among the cows, and reconstructed the takeaway. He explained: "I wanted to see myself take the club back more in one piece."

Ballesteros also began exercising on a 'Gravity Gym' machine, a fixed trapese device with pads and canvas loops which he had first seen the previous autumn in Graham Marsh's home in Perth, Australia. Three sessions a day the Spaniard dangled from the device, twisting and lifting himself as many as forty times a session, stretching and building the muscles of his imperfect back.

On rare departures from Pedreña, Ballesteros dated a television presenter in Barcelona. It was through her that he met a psychiatrist interested in what the Spanish call 'sufrologia', a form of positive thinking. A 30-minute cassette tape was made in which the doctor's soothing voice speaks to Seve who listens through a plug in his ear. "What the doctor says to me is private," Ballesteros says. "But it helps me to relax and convinces me I am good."

Sound in body and mind, Ballesteros now turned to the heart of the game, especially at Augusta: putting. Augusta's greens could be harrowingly fast, he knew, but apart from household carpets there was only one fast surface at hand: the Pedreña beach, with the tide out. The beach wasn't as undulating as Augusta's greens, but that

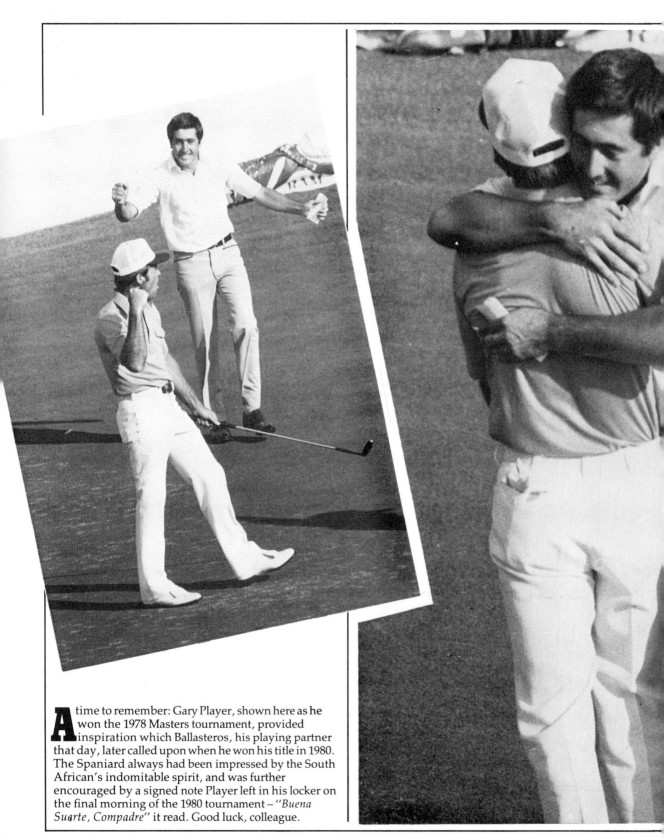

A time to remember: Gary Player, shown here as he won the 1978 Masters tournament, provided inspiration which Ballasteros, his playing partner that day, later called upon when he won his title in 1980. The Spaniard always had been impressed by the South African's indomitable spirit, and was further encouraged by a signed note Player left in his locker on the final morning of the 1980 tournament – "*Buena Suarte, Compadre*" it read. Good luck, colleague.

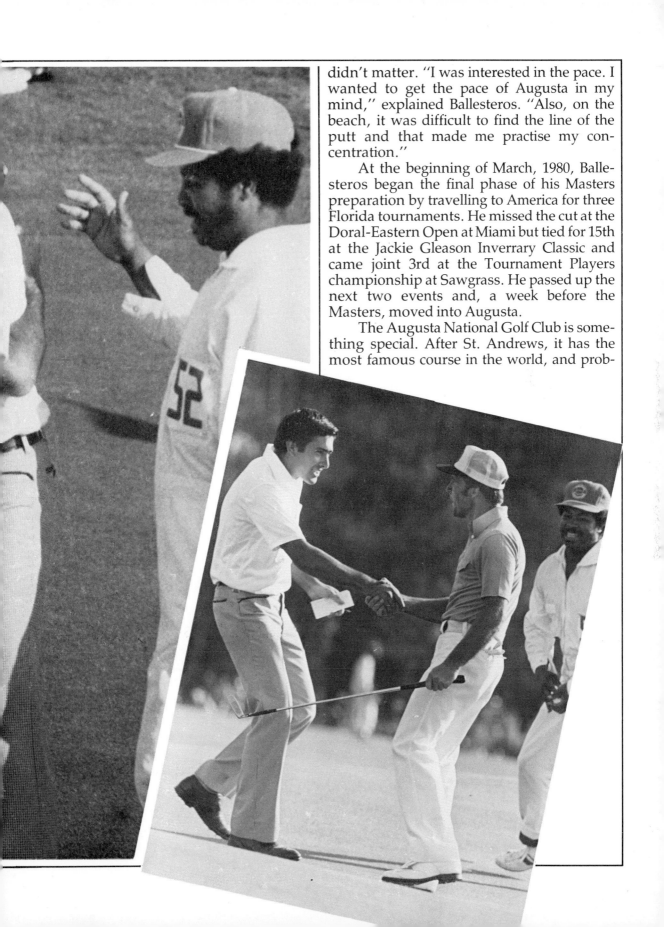

didn't matter. "I was interested in the pace. I wanted to get the pace of Augusta in my mind," explained Ballesteros. "Also, on the beach, it was difficult to find the line of the putt and that made me practise my concentration."

At the beginning of March, 1980, Ballesteros began the final phase of his Masters preparation by travelling to America for three Florida tournaments. He missed the cut at the Doral-Eastern Open at Miami but tied for 15th at the Jackie Gleason Inverrary Classic and came joint 3rd at the Tournament Players championship at Sawgrass. He passed up the next two events and, a week before the Masters, moved into Augusta.

The Augusta National Golf Club is something special. After St. Andrews, it has the most famous course in the world, and prob-

Play it again, Seve: The Spaniard, in disagreement with the referee, drops twice from the creek on the 13th fairway, then stalks away on the last day of the 1980 Masters.

87

ably the finest one inland. It certainly is the most colourful, with 65 stately magnolias that march up the long drive to the clubhouse and blazing azalea, yellow jasmine and other pungent flowers and trees that lend their names to holes. The fairways are invitingly broad, the greens enormous and subtly-contoured, as one might expect of such an admirer of British seaside links as Bobby Jones, who devised Augusta. With no rough to speak of and only 44 bunkers, the most dangerous natural hazards are the flowering dogwood and the longlead pines.

Ballesteros's first problem in 1980 was to 'get his distances' – that is, to pace off the distances from landmarks, such as an isolated tree or sprinkler head, to the fronts and backs of greens. In the past the distances had been got by his regular caddy, Marion Herrington, but Herrington got them in yards. Ballesteros, a Continental European, thinks in metres, and he would have to add 10 percent to convert the yards to metres. Such mental arithmetic was imprecise and wasted time. Yards wouldn't do in 1980. Ballesteros therefore paced off his own distances and entered them into a booklet he kept in his hip pocket.

Next Ballesteros studied placement of his tee shots. All Augusta's holes, save perhaps the second, are reachable in two shots and most are doglegs; therefore, a high premium is placed on playing into a position that 'opens up' a green. To this end it is important at Augusta to 'think a hole backwards'. Nicklaus does. On practice days, he can be seen at the front of greens, staring back over the rolling waves of fairway, considering where his approach shot should come from. Ballesteros did the same.

Ballesteros finally studied the greens. Augusta's are not only big and racy but they hump and roll and fall away in the most frightening manner. A downhill putt, merely touched, can run off the green. "In practice," Ballesteros said later, "I spent much time looking for places where I could putt uphill at a hole." The Spaniard also noted that the greens, after a wet spring, were slowish for Augusta. Some were notably slower than others.

Ballesteros was ready. Publically, he would make no predictions. Privately, he was bubbling with confidence. "Give me a three-stroke lead with three holes to play," he told a friend, referring to Sneed's collapse in 1979, "and I'll win."

On the afternoon before the first round, Nicklaus customarily calls together the world's press to explain his and Augusta's current form. This time Watson, Nicklaus's heir presumptive, beat him to it. Watson called *his* press conference. The Kansas Citian's press conferences, while less patronising, are every bit as informed as Nicklaus's. Watson felt he was in good form, except in one department: "My driving's a hair-line off."

As for Augusta, the recent weather had left the fairways and greens 'a little bit skinny' of their usual lush growth but the soft course would play long. The usual key holes, the par 5s, were therefore even more crucial this year but, for Watson, the biggest psychological hurdle came at the 14th, not one of Augusta's usually remarked holes, but one that immediately follows the tensions of Amen Corner, the trio of tough holes at the far end of the course. You could pay dearly by emotionally relaxing on fourteen. He felt the most interesting hole this year was the new 8th. Because of the new contouring of the approaches to the green, the course was now one-third of a shot tougher than in 1979. The field was strong, however, and he estimated the winning score would be 278, ten under par and slightly below the average over the past decade.

Who would win? Such big hitters as Andy Bean and Ballesteros – and Nicklaus, 'because he knows where to hit the ball round here' – must be favourites. What, Watson wondered aloud, was the line from London? The British press dutifully found out: Ladbrokes fancied Watson at 5 to 1, followed by Nicklaus at 8 to 1 and Ballesteros at 12 to 1.

Watson's puzzling remark about the 'new' 8th hole adding 'a third of a stroke' to the course bears expansion. To the casual visitor, the Augusta National course appears sacrosanct. It isn't. In an effort to keep up with the improvements in the game over the past thirty years, the ground staff had made well over 150 alterations, a remarkable number in the conservative world of golf. A tee has been elevated here, a bunker shifted there, greens relocated and recontoured, ponds dug and filled, trees cut down and replanted. "I don't know a course in the world, except maybe Nicklaus's at Muirfield Village," Watson once said, "that undergoes such regular revision as the Augusta National."

And so it was with the eighth. The hole, 530 yards long, mostly uphill and bending left past a colourful wood, had shown up on the computer the previous year as the easiest par 5 at Augusta. Something had to be done. The job, as usual, was left to the Tournament Improvements Committee, a powerful body which includes such former Masters winners as Gene Sarazen, Ben Hogan and Byron Nelson.

The problem was easy to identify, and no one saw it more clearly than Nelson. In the old days – before 1956 – the green had been guarded by three massive mounds rolling back along the left from off the green. If the ambitious shot was overdrawn, and if the flag was tucked back left, a player was set the difficult task of approaching over the mounds for a crack at the flag. What is more, three smaller mounds had guarded the approach on the right front of the green, creating a flattish bowl.

"It was one of the most unusual greens I ever played, and one of the most challenging," says Nelson, who in 1942 effectively won his second Masters with a play-off eagle 3 there against Ben Hogan. "If you were accurate you could use the mounds. If you weren't, they could use you." In 1956 the mounds were removed to allow spectators a better view down the fairway from behind the green. "Without those mounds," Nelson goes on, "you could hit just about any old shot off the fairway, as long as you stayed out of the trees." After the 1979 Masters the Committee decided the green area had to be restored to its original configuration and, working from plastic models, the job was done through the summer. By 1980, as almost always, the course was just a little different for the Masters.

The opening day dawned clear and bright, with a maurauding breeze, but not enough sun to warrant the white peaked cap Ballesteros wore when he appeared on the first tee at 12.12. Frankly, he looked odd. The cap, obscuring those dark, expressive eyes, muted his glamour. He wore it for reasons: to block out gallery distractions and, more cunningly, to reduce the glare of Augusta's crystalline white bunker sand. He was dressed conservatively in a white shirt and dark blue trousers. "I feel calm in calm colours," he says. "I don't want people to watch me the way I dress. I want people to watch me the way I play."

As the 1979 Open champion, Ballesteros was playing the star role in his pairing. His partner was Craig Stadler, 'the Walrus', a corpulent, irritable American with a drooping moustache. In past years, Ballesteros had set out, all guns blazing, aiming his big drive over the corner of a distant bunker and, perilously, played hide-and-seek with a stand of pine trees out to the right. This year, having noticed how Trevino played the hole, he settled into his stance, slightly closer than usual to the ball, aimed down the left side of the fairway and, gently swinging in an outside-inside plane, faded his drive into the middle of the fairway. A crisp pitch, two putts, and the Spaniard was away with a par.

Ballesteros was a model of wise, easy power throughout the round, missing only one fairway off the tee – in contrast to his fabled last round in the 1979 Open at Lytham where he hit only two – and when he erred he did not strike back as he might have done in the old days. He probably never played a more impressive round in his life. At the end of the day, his 66, six under par, shared the lead with the Australian David Graham, who reigned as American PGA champion, and Jeff Mitchell who, as a West Texan, ought to have played well in the wind. The favourite Watson played without distinction for a 73 and Nicklaus, troubled by the wind, scored a 74.

The weather on the second day was blissfully bright, with barely a breeze. Ballesteros was paired with Larry Nelson whom, in the 1979 Ryder Cup matches, he had called lucky to hole a long chip shot. The American team and press had made a meal of this careless remark. After Lytham, they felt, who was calling whom lucky? At Augusta, neither man would rekindle the fuel for the press. They played with friendly, mutual respect.

The Spaniard's golf that day was pure theatre. At moments it was the old Ballesteros: he jumped at the odd ball, sending it screaming off line, then punished these mistakes with great, lashing recoveries. He scored birdies off his three most hideous drives of the day, the last one worse, by acres, than his fabled 'parking lot' drive at Lytham.

The build-up to that nightmare drive began on the fifteenth when, subduing the 520-yard hole with a drive and a 3-iron, he scored a birdie. It put him nine strokes under par, three clear of his nearest pursuer, Graham, who had just reached the sixth tee. Pumped up with adrenalin, Ballesteros called for his 8-iron as he stepped on to the tee of the watery, 190-yard sixteenth. "No," said Herrington, "It's a little 7-iron." Ballesteros relented and pounded his ball eighty feet past the pin, leaving himself an ugly downhill putt. As he left the tee, a nearby explosion of applause signalled Graham's birdie on the sixth green. Ballesteros three-putted to fall back to a single stroke advantage over the Australian.

Herrington was horrified by his mistake. He apologised to Ballesteros. The Spaniard, eschewing the tenet by which he always shifts the blame away from himself, replied, "Don't worry. It was my fault." Ballesteros was seething with himself when he reached the 17th tee. He snap-hooked his drive. The ball veered left, clicked through the top of a pine tree, bounced into the adjacent seventh fairway, skipped between a pair of bunkers and ran up on to the elevated seventh green. It came to rest some ten feet from the hole – the wrong hole.

Ballesteros climbed to the green where he met Graham and his playing partner, Andy North. The situation was bizarre. Here was the Spaniard, ten holes ahead of his nearest rival, on the same green. What's more, Ballesteros's ball was in Graham's direct line to the hole. "Nice drive," said Graham. "Would you like to play through?" Ballesteros, embarrassed, marked his ball and, as soon as the green cleared, dropped clear without penalty. Once, twice the ball rolled away and finally Ballesteros set it in place.

He surveyed the prospect before him. Clearly, such a shot had never before been contemplated in the 46-year history of the Masters: high over the corner of a massive scoreboard, over a gigantic hump and on to a hidden green. In all, 150 yards. Crowds were cleared from behind the green. Spectators, blundering across the path of the shot, were startled to be shouted back. Many cowered, scattered. "Are you going to make a birdie?" a fan asked. "Yes," said Seve.

The Spaniard took a precarious footing and smashed his 7-iron shot over the edge of the scoreboard, crouched and listened. Silence. Then deafening, distant applause. Ballesteros was away, half-sprinting after it, his fans surging behind him. It was Palmer in the 60s, all over again. "Waa-hoo!" Then from one Southern throat came the curious drawl, *"Olé!"*

Ballesteros found the ball only fifteen feet from the hole and, smooth as milk from a pitcher, he poured in the putt for the birdie he had promised. Nelson, bemused, later remembered the Spaniard, a fixed look in his eye, marching toward the final tee. "When Seve gets going he starts walking fast, he's got different thoughts on his mind," Nelson commented. "Seve is a rare kind of guy. He's an excitable golfer who can concentrate."

The pyrotechnics were done for the day. Ballesteros scored an untroubled par on the finishing hole for a 69 and a midway total of 135, which put him four strokes clear of the field. In his wake, on 139, lay Graham and Rex Caldwell, a journeyman American. The two giants of the game looked lost in the crowd, Watson on 142 after another 71; Nicklaus on 145, also having returned a 71, a total that by only a single stroke escaped the 36-hole cut.

Nelson, after scoring a workaday 72 with

Ballesteros, reckoned that Watson and the Spaniard were heirs-apparent to Nicklaus. He compared and contrasted these two princes of golf. "Tom and Seve are totally different in their attitude," he said. "Tom is more involved in technique and perfecting his swing. It's in the back of his mind to score well, sure, but what he's concerned about is hitting the ball perfectly as a means to this end. Seve is different. He just wants to shoot lower scores than anybody else."

There had been lower 36-hole Masters scores shot than Ballesteros's – Raymond Floyd's 131 in 1976 was the lowest – but on only three occasions had players held a more commanding lead at this point: Floyd in 1976, Nicklaus in 1975 and Herman Keiser in 1946 – all were five strokes clear of their fields. The Spaniard was set fair. "Seve is going to have to be caught," said Graham. "I don't think he will back up."

The Masters was now taking shape: unless someone mounted an attack and kept pressure on him, the confident Ballesteros might turn on the steam and, like a distance runner or cyclist, break away from the field. The weather, only a mild wind and enough rain to soften the green, prophesied low enough scores for such an attack to succeed. It would be a fascinating day.

Gibby Gilbert, nine strokes behind, made the first move. He birdied four of the

A wire service photograph, showing Ballesteros's caddie jumping in despair as Seve's putt misses the 5th hole in the third round at Augusta.

MASTERS
AUPOH1212-4/12/80-AUGUSTA, GA.: Seve Ballesteros's caddie leaps off the ground in disappointment after the Spaniard's ball(lower right)failed to drop on the fifth green. It was one of the few of Ballesteros's putts that didn't drop... he holds a commanding lead of the Masters 4/12 with a 12-under par game.
JLs/SAM PARRISH
UPI

first seven holes before Ballesteros teed off, closing the gap to five strokes. In itself, this was not worrying, for Gilbert still had the more difficult home half of the course to play. But who next might make a run at the Spaniard?

Ballesteros opened the day with rickety bogie-birdie-bogie-par then hoiked an ungainly drive, 'almost between my legs' off the 5th and straight into a stand of pines. As luck had it, the ball came to rest precisely where the ground staff had recently uprooted a tree. Only Seve could have found such a place. If on the previous day the Spaniard, after dropping off the seventh green, played a shot no man ever had played before in the Masters, his ball lay this time where no player had ever trod: in the rough in the little valley at the bottom of the sixth fairway and, as he faced the unseen and faraway fifth green, hard against a rising wall of pine trees.

Ballesteros, nearly 250 yards from the green, could not play towards it. "Seve, maybe here you are going to take a double-bogie 6," he said to himself. "But even if you do, you're still going to be one shot ahead. Keep calm. Don't get mad."

Calmly, Ballesteros selected a pitching wedge, opened the face flat, and with a vicious slash sent his ball climbing steeply over the trees and back into the fairway. A long pitch and two putts later and Ballesteros had a 5, possibly the most satisfying bogie he had scored in his life. Nonetheless, his lead was now only two strokes from Graham, his playing partner who birdied the hole, and Caldwell.

Ballesteros is most dangerous when wounded, and on the next hole, a par 3 that drops like a stone to a wildly rolling green, he nearly scored a hole-in-one. His 7-iron shot off the 190-yard hole, pitched nicely short of the flag, ran up and twitched away from the cup for an easy birdie 2. He was back in command, three strokes in front; yet he had scored only one par in his six holes for the day.

In retrospect, many holes appear crucial in the winning of a tournament but none, even during what was to be an eventful final day, could have been more important to Ballesteros's Masters victory than the 8th on the third day. The 8th – where the green was re-modelled by Byron Nelson; Ballesteros came into it after parring the 7th.

As the Spaniard walked towards the tee his confidence returned: glancing up at the big scoreboard he had seen that Watson almost certainly was gone. The American had bogied the 11th, had taken a triple-bogie 6 on the short 12th (by blocking his tee shot into Rae's Creek) and lay ten strokes behind him. Graham was now 4 back, Caldwell 3.

Ballesteros cracked a big drive, 285 yards and nearly all carry. He could not see the green from his ball but, consulting his hip booklet, he reckoned the pin to be 224 metres (245 yards) away, almost all uphill. He walked forward, had a look and took a decision. He wouldn't bother shaping his shot off the mounds; he'd just fly it string-straight, covering the flag all the way. And that's what he did: struck a stupendous 3-iron, high and straight. The ball dropped light as a feather on to the green, and came to rest six feet from the hole. Seve stroked in the putt for an eagle 3.

The effect of the 3-iron blow was devastating. Graham who over the past few holes had appeared to be playing slowly in an intentional attempt to break the Spaniard's pace, was shattered. He dropped a shot on the hole and was not heard of again. With that eagle to help him, Ballesteros made the turn in 35; one under par, and playing with almost unremarkable brilliance he came home in 33 for a round of 68. This put him at 203, distantly followed by the chubby American Ed Fiori, who had come in with a 69 for a 210 total. Graham, 72, was in joint third spot, along with Newton, Andy North, the 1978 US Open Champion, and J. C. Snead, the legendary Sam's nephew, all on 211.

The 1980 Masters seemed over bar the shouting, and the counting. With a seven-stroke lead and standing thirteen under par, Ballesteros had raised prospects of a record victory. He could not only become the youngest man ever to win the Masters, being eighty days younger than Nicklaus was when he triumphed in 1963, but he could join the exalted company of Nicklaus, Francis Ouimet and Bobby Jones as the only men in history to win two or more major championships by the age of 23. Further, the Spaniard could set another record by winning by a wider margin than Nicklaus's nine strokes in 1965.

Not surprisingly, Ballesteros said he would first see to his victory before taking on other targets. Seve, no doubt about it, was stuffing the Yanks in their own back yard, and the foreign players rallied round him. From the blunt, warm-hearted Newton, who was to be paired on the final day with the Spaniard, came a surprisingly virulent defence in a broadside delivered over television.

"I've read some of the newspaper articles this week and, you know, it's almost as though you guys are waiting for Seve to blow it," snapped Newton, glaring at the camera. "I've also heard some pretty snide, completely uncalled-for remarks from some of the players. They say he's lucky and a 'one-putt Jessie' and all that (bleep) . . . America's considered to be the tops in professional golf and here comes a young 23-year-old and he's taken some of the highlight away from your superstars. But, you know, the guy's a great player and the sooner Americans realize it the better." With that, Newton turned and went back to the putting green.

Ballesteros looked remarkably composed. "Come to dinner," he said to a journalist from London. "Only we don't talk about golf, okay?" He had invited eight friends to dinner, mostly Spanish, mostly male. He does not seek attention but when later he appeared in the living room of his rented house, dressed in a yellow shirt, all eyes drifted to him. Ballesteros radiated golf that night although there was only a single golfing item in the room: an antique, hickory-shafted putter which lay on the otherwise empty coffee table: a birthday gift to Seve from Rhena Barner, Ed's wife. Guests wandered by, however, and as though it was a talisman which had been blessed by genius they picked it up, waggled it and looked askance at Ballesteros.

It was a buffet dinner and towards a pretty female American journalist, much lib-erated, he was courtly, guiding her through the queue and putting her firmly at the head of the table. Towards Señor Jose Santiuste, the elderly gentleman to whom he had given his 1979 Open championship ball, he was deferential. Among his fellows, he was lusty and jovial – they indulged in great teasing of accents, and made much play of *cojones*, the Spanish measure of courage.

One minute Ballesteros was joking about Spanish football – the national team had recently been thrashed by England – the next he was watching *Saturday Night Fever* on television in the den, quite outside the mainstream of conversation. Then he was gone. It was 10 o'clock. He lay on his bed, the cassette ear-piece plugged into his ear, listening to the soothing words of the Barcelona psychiatrist.

13 April, the fourth day, and Ballesteros and Newton appeared on the first tee prepared to drive off at 1.48. Seve started in irrepressible form. With the most delicate of pitches he birdied the first, then the third hole, to increase his lead to ten strokes.

At about that time Jim Armstrong II, the club manager, was in his office with Seve's manager. What size Green Jacket would Ballesteros require? 42, Regular. In the certain belief that such a standard size could be borrowed from the pro shop, Armstrong went on to explain the rights and responsibilities surrounding the Green Jacket. A new champion was entitled to wear it off the Augusta National Golf Club premises only for his tenure as champion and only at social golfing functions. Thereafter it would be kept for him in a cedar-lined closet in the champions' locker room. Ballesteros would have permanent privileges to that locker room. Armstrong had begun to itemise the other prizes that would come to Ballesteros: the $55,000 first prize, of course, and a silver humidor bearing the signatures of all the players. Crystal vases for low daily scores, Thursday and Friday; a pair of crystal goblets for the eagle . . . then news came from the course. Ballesteros was falling apart.

The Spaniard had played cast-iron golf since the fifth and made the turn in 33 to go sixteen under par for the tournament and ten

clear of Newton – and of Gilbert, who was moving down the eleventh fairway. As the young Spaniard stood on the tenth tee the low-lying holes beneath him must have looked like El Dorado.

The golden vision soon turned to dross. On the 10th green, a speedy theadbare surface, Ballesteros 3-putted and Newton, with a par, closed the gap to nine strokes. Ballesteros righted himself on the 11th, but Newton birdied. Eight strokes. The Spaniard thought – almost nonchalantly – that his chance of breaking the tournament record of 271 strokes was slipping. ¿y que? so what? Augusta's 12th is 'the most demanding tournament hole in the world', according to Nicklaus. A one-shotter at only 155 yards, it is tucked at the end of the famed Amen Corner, just over Rae's Creek, and against a tall backcloth of pine trees. Winds coming down the course glance and swirl off this backcloth, and players standing on a sheltered tee have no way of reading the air currents high above the green. A well-struck shot can abruptly hold up and drop like a stone into a bunker in front of the green or, worse, into the creek.

Year after year, Masters aspirations drown in the creek. 1980 was no exception. A triple bogie had finished Watson's hopes on the previous day and Weiskopf, en route to his 85 on the opening day, had put five balls in the creek, an all-time record, and taken 13 on the hole. The Spaniard studied the heaving pines in the distance and planned his shot: he would start his ball left and let the wind bring it into the flag.

He set himself solidly, aiming left, and took his 6-iron into the backswing. At the top of his swing a thought suddenly struck him: *go straight for the pin*. As his club started down, it happened: his leading hand, the left one, tightened on the grip. He fractionally let up, 'blocked-out', and the ball flew to the right.

Ballesteros watched, feeling helpless as the ball pitched into the bank, stuck, then trickled down into the creek. There was no

calling it back. The Spaniard, who rarely swears, did so now. Electing to drop out of the water under one stroke penalty, Ballesteros meticulously dropped the ball over his shoulder in the correct line between the flag and the point at which the ball entered the water. He chipped to the back of the green, just to be safe, and carefully two-putted. A double-bogie 5. Newton took another birdie: the three-stroke swing closed Ballesteros's gap to five strokes. It was a comfortable enough lead, but one that was moving alarmingly in the wrong direction.

Off the next, elevated tee, Ballesteros punished his drive, drawing it nicely round the dogleg. From there, he pondered the shot: 162 metres (180 yards) over Rae's Creek which at that point lay crooked in front of the green. A 4-iron? The choice struck him as dangerous; he needed more club. He called for his 3-iron. Herrington felt it was wrong but said nothing. Ballesteros thought: hit the ball softly, get control of your power again.

His decision was disastrous. Swinging unnaturally slowly, Ballesteros hit the ball 'fat': that is, he struck the turf a full two inches too far behind the ball. The clubhead dug in. The ball climbed feebly into the air, fell short of the green and skipped into the creek. Walking up the fairway, Ballesteros felt the eyes of the crowd on him; suddenly he experienced the same sense of embattlement that he had witnessed in Player on the same fairway in 1978. *These people don't think I can win. I'll show them.* He lifted out of the water, as he had done on the previous hole, and dropped the ball over his shoulder. The referee asked him to drop it again. *This man is trying to put me off!* thought Ballesteros, and he lost his temper.

"Sir", he snapped sarcastically, "Are you *sure*, sir?" Yes, the referee was sure. Ballesteros dropped again. His chip was once again safely strong but, putting back down a slope, he hit the hole and the ball snapped away. He finished it off for a bogie 6 – against *another* Newton birdie, his third on the trot – and the Spaniard's lead was down to three strokes. Meanwhile applause mushroomed up ahead: Gilbert had birdied the 14th hole; the American was now four strokes behind

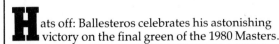

H ats off: Ballesteros celebrates his astonishing victory on the final green of the 1980 Masters.

At the victory ceremony, Ballesteros sits with his nearest challenger. *Left to right*: Gibby Gilbert and Jack Newton.

---

and closing in. You are *stupid*, Ballesteros said to himself. What are you doing? You were comfortable but now you are in trouble. You can lose this tournament. You must work hard.

Newton cracked a perfect drive up the fourteenth fairway. Ballesteros hooked his. The ball swerved left into trees. At that point, a curious incident took place as Ballesteros moved up the fairway. A spectator shouted at him, point-blank: "Come on, Jack! Go, Jack!" The image of a rampaging Nicklaus came into the Spaniard's mind. It did not occur to him that the man might be shouting in support of Jack Newton.

"The shout was like a knife in the heart for me," Ballesteros recalls. "I looked at the man and made a big expression in my eyes. The crowd, the referee – and now this guy. I didn't know whether people were against me or not, but that was how I felt and, let me tell you, it helped. I am like Gary Player. The more the crowd is against me, the more I want to prove something."

Ballesteros's shot needed shaping and with a 6-iron he shaped it perfectly round a tree, over a greenside mound and into the green, twenty-five feet past the flag. It was a glorious stroke, one that Newton later said won the Spaniard the Masters. Ballesteros nearly ran in the putt for a birdie, but settled happily for a par. It left him three ahead of Newton and, as news drifted back, also three ahead of Gilbert, who had just birdied the fifteenth hole.

Augusta's fifteenth, a par 5 of 520 yards, travels over a lumpy fairway which, just beyond the driving area, falls away to a pond in front of a sloping, elevated green. It is a fine, frightening hole, the frequent scene of competitors, trouser-leg rolled, knee-deep in water. The tee itself presents a view of half of Georgia.

Ballesteros smashed a 310-yard drive to the perfect position, the right-centre of the fairway. "Give me a birdie and we can take it home," said his caddie. The Spaniard selected a 4-iron, an ambitious club with water just short of the green, and gave the ball a mighty lash. He hit it fat, as he had so calamitously done on the thirteenth fairway. Herrington muttered, "Good shot, sir," which sounded

strange to the Spaniard.

Herrington was right. It was a good shot, settling softly down on the green, inside Newton's ball, and some twenty feet from the pin. As Ballesteros reached the green he lifted his hand to the applause and glanced at the scoreboard. Herrington, he thought, wasn't right this time: a birdie here might not take home the title. Gilbert had birdied the 16th to draw within two shots of the Spaniard.

Newton putted first. His stroke, on Ballesteros's line, sped eight feet past the hole. It not only showed the Spaniard the way, it also showed the green to be dangerously fast. Accordingly, Ballesteros played a cozy tap. Even so the ball limped on and on, four feet past the hole. Newton, playing first, missed his return putt. Ballesteros put his down. A birdie, against Newton's par, lifted him four clear of the Australian, three of Gilbert. *Give me a three-stroke lead with three holes to play*, he remembered saying on the eve of the tournament, *and I'll win the Masters*.

All that now stood between him and the title, the Spaniard felt, was the sixteenth, where water stretches nearly the whole way from tee to green. For safety, he drilled a firm 6-iron past the pin. Then he gently tapped the first putt, holed the second. "It's finished," he said, turning to his caddy. "The tournament is ours."

It was. Ballesteros, keeping an eye on the scoreboard, cruised safely into port. He scored two solid pars on the home holes, to finish with 72 for the day and 275 for the tournament, three under Watson's forecast. At 23 years and four days, Ballesteros was the youngest Master of them all.

Try that for size: Ballesteros helped on with the winner's Green Jacket by the 1979 victor, Fuzzy Zoeller.

Shaping your Shots

Augusta, with all those fairways bending from right to left, is laid out for a player who can draw the ball. Lee Trevino, of course, fades it from left to right on nearly all his shots. Therefore it is strange but true that I learned the value of shaping my shots while playing a practice round with Lee at the Masters.

The idea struck home, as we saw in the last chapter, on the first tee. There is awful trouble, I know first hand, to the right of the fairway, and in practice I noticed Lee setting up and aiming down the left side. He wasn't just playing away from trouble. He was opening up the entire width of the fairway because he knew, with his dependable fade, that by starting his ball left it would finish in the fairway.

I will take this idea one step further. You should *never* aim your shots straight at the pin, unless you are playing the short irons, say from the 7 through to the pitching wedge. The reason I write this is that few players, even the best, can hit a ball dead straight every time. When you attempt to hit a perfectly straight ball it will almost certainly drift to the left, in a draw, or to the right in a fade. That means, by lining your shot straight down the fairway or towards the pin, you are reducing your landing area exactly by half. Also, you are in danger of not finishing on the choice side of the fairway, faced with a difficult shot towards the green or the pin.

It is much better to fade or draw your shots into the flag; choose the one you control best. As for me, I can control the fade a little more with the woods and long irons, and the draw with the middle irons. If you can fade or draw your shots at will, you can play your ball through the safe way to the green. Also, this is very important: an intentional fade or draw gives you more 'feel' and control than an absolutely straight shot.

In conclusion, always feel and see the shape of your shot in your mind and, unless it is a little one into the pin, *never* think straight.

Master's tip: Lee Trevino slides through a drive on the first tee at Augusta

CHAPTER EIGHT

A REIGN IN SPAIN, FOLLOWED BY DROUGHT

"This is a driver" [holds up club to viewers], "and this is a putter."

Manuel Piñero, explaining golf on Spanish national television.

In California, two days after the Masters, Ballesteros reported to the players' registration desk to pick up his credentials for the Tournament of Champions at Rancho la Costa. He searched through the envelope and looked up in surprise. "Something is missing," he said to the lady behind the desk. "Where is my identification badge?"

The lady clapped her hands in front of her face, charmed. "You don't need a badge, Seve," she replied. "*Everybody* knows who you are." Indeed, everybody in America seemed to know Seve. He had chatted the previous morning on a nationwide television show and already his handsome face had appeared on the cover of *Sports Illustrated*. Bob Hope asked him to play a round with him and Muhammad Ali phoned to call him 'The Greatest'. A tide of telegrams, including *felicitaciones* from King Juan Carlos and Adolfo Suarez of Spain, poured in from around the world. In the church at Pedreña, where Seve once served as a choir boy, bells pealed through the night when news came of his victory and the sexton, also the village poet, sat down to compose an 'Ode to Severiano Ballesteros'.

Yet to say the Spaniard was a prophet without honour in his own country is not far wrong. "The newspapers will say that Balle-steros won the Masters and that will be about it," Seve said, without much rancour, at a press conference that week in California. "Television will get round to showing the highlights in a few months – on the second national channel." Indeed, in the eyes of most Spaniards Ballesteros was no celebrity, certainly no El Cordobes, Alfredo Di Stefano or Manuel Santana. A Reuters report from Madrid told of the nation's reaction to Ballesteros's victory. Spanish Radio began a news bulletin with a new national swimming record and failed to mention Ballesteros at all. A Madrid restaurateur, famed for the sports photographs that decorate his dining rooms, received the news with two words: "Who? . . . What?" A Spanish Golf Federation official commented in turn: "Such a reaction comes as no surprise."

Ballesteros is a *golfista*, and since there are only 25,000 native *golfistas* in Spain, a nation of some 36 million people, his sport is about as popular as, say, fencing in Britain or cricket in the United States. Further, it is the sport of the foreign tourist or the Spanish rich: of its 76 courses only a couple of dozen are open to the public, and even then only if the player is a member of the Spanish Golf Federation.

What is more, at the time of Ballesteros's classic triumph there were just 248 registered members of the Spanish Professional Golfers' Association. Of these only a dozen were also members of the Tournament Players' Division of the British PGA and, as such, eligible to

World champions: Ballesteros, with his teammate Manuel Pinero, captures the 1976 World Cup for Spain, a trophy which many of their countrymen considered the most important in golf.

compete regularly on the British and Continental circuit. Again: of these fifteen only one was committed to world travel – Ballesteros. Spain's power in world golf, despite its few professionals, is remarkable. That it should have won World Cups in 1976 and 1977 – with Seve, it should be stressed, by no means carrying the load alone – is no real measure of their might: two good players from any among several countries, enjoying a purple patch, would be capable of winning. Spain's strength lies in a depth of only about six world-class players; if one were to enlarge the national teams to perhaps half a dozen players it is probable that Spain could beat

every nation in the world, save the United States, but including England, Scotland, South Africa, Japan and possibly Australia.

Spain's excellence in golf is one of the phenomena of sport. Much has to do with the opportunities it offers to the hungry youngsters – hungry both literally and figuratively – who are reared round the nation's exclusive clubs. Golf is their way out of poverty, much as young American Blacks and Puerto Ricans see their escape through boxing. Also – and paradoxically, since skill so often flowers in fields of adversity – the extremely high standards of courses in Spain have helped in the development of its young professional players.

Spain has the finest courses on the Continent. They are mostly sheltered from the cold assaults of weather. They are big layouts, kept in immaculate condition and, in the

American manner, well-watered. The greens are soft and true, the fairway turf lush and uniform. All of this makes for good holiday golf, a chief function of Spanish courses; it also encourages a carefree, attacking game which develops confidence and, not least, the grooved swing that has become the hallmark of the top Spanish players. To learn 'fiddly' manufactured shots, as Ballesteros and Trevino did in their childhoods, is useful in times of trouble. To build an entire round on artificial shot-making, as the luckless Scots have been compelled to do down the generations, is something else.

The crucial importance of courses to Spanish golfers was once discussed by the wise British Ryder Cup player, Dai Rees. He compared the backgrounds of Spanish and British players in this respect. "I think it would be possible to tip the scales in Britain's favour if it could be arranged for about a dozen of our best young professionals to be taken to spend a whole winter – from the end of October right through to the end of March – in Spain," he wrote in Britain's *Golf Monthly* of October 1976. "To play on those long Spanish courses which are so good, to play in almost the same weather conditions every day, to play consistently from good fairway lies, and so develop one golf swing for all the shots they have to play."

The history of Spanish golf is short and, at first, not even concerned with Spaniards. The country's first club, Club de Golf de las Palmas, was founded in the Canary Islands in 1891 and catered almost exclusively for tourists, mostly British. The game did not move to the mainland until 1904 with the layout of a course on the grounds of the Madrid Polo Club. Then, in 1914, the club moved and, granted the seal of approval by His Majesty King Alfonso XIII, became the Real Club de la Puerta de Hierro. In prestige it has become something like St. Andrews in Britain.

By then France was far down the fairway of Continental golf. Her first club, Pau in the Pyrenees, founded in 1854, was already more than a half century old. France had held her first Amateur championship (1900) and her first Open (1906) both at La Boulie, near Ver-

sailles. Best of all, apart from Britain or America, France produced the world's first great player: Arnauld Massy. If not a Spaniard Massy was the nearest thing to it. He was a French Basque, born in Biarritz, only a few miles from the Spanish border. A natural left-hander, Massy was converted to the orthodox right side when he went as a young man to seek his fame and fortune in North Berwick, in Scotland. By then Berwick was long established as a golfing resort, frequented by such statesmen as A. J. Balfour, the future Prime Minister. Massy was soon enjoying widespread acclaim.

A huge man with a great balletic swing that began and ended with him on the tips of his toes, Massy won the inaugural French Open in 1906. At Hoylake the following year he left his mark in the record book as the only Continental, before Ballesteros, to win the Open. That 1907 Open, interestingly, was the first covered by the most famous of all golf writers, Bernard Darwin. Darwin reported that Massy led the qualifiers in 'bad weather' with a fine 73–74, then in a 'very trying' wind moved to the head of the championship field with a 76–81 after the opening day.

"Massy, although he holed some long puts (*sic*), took three puts on several greens," Darwin wrote of the Frenchman's following two rounds of 78 and 77. "The rest of his golf was very steady." The victory was achieved in strong company, for among those vanquished were the Triumvirate of Vardon, Taylor and Braid.

Massy's impact on Spanish golf was to be profound, for he triumphed in the first Spanish Open, held in 1912 at Puerta de Hierro, and again over the same course in 1927 and 1928. By then there were only nine courses in Spain, the most recent being the royally chartered one – on ground that once belonged to Ballesteros' forbears at Pedreña.

Massy died in 1958 at the age of 81. By then the baton of Continental golf had long

Alumnus Piñero, the Spaniard overshadowed only by Ballesteros, returns to the caddie school at Club de Campo, Madrid, where he studied, caddied and learned the game as a boy.

been in the firm grasp of a Belgian, Flory Van Donck. Van Donck, an elegant and courtly strokemaker, was the foremost mainland European golfer for over twenty years, winning the Dutch Open as early as 1936 and coming second to Gary Player in the 1959 Open at Muirfield.

Spanish golf was interrupted by her Civil War (1936–39) – during which, most notably, the course at Puerta de Hierro was destroyed. It also interrupted the career of her first fine player, Angel Miguel. Born in 1921, son of a poor labourer in Madrid, Miguel scratched out a living as a caddy at Puerta de Hierro. He was joined after the Civil War by his younger brother, Sebastian, born in 1929. As caddies, they were barred from the course, but, in the tradition of future Spanish caddies, they dug out practice holes outside the rough. The Miguels came to notice in the late 1940s when the great eccentric British golfer, Max Faulkner, gave exhibitions at Puerta de Hierro.

"They were still caddies then, skinny, under-fed chappies in string-soled shoes," recalls Faulkner. Yet in a couple of years the Miguels had become formidable players. "From a distance Angel was a double for Ben Hogan – same tidy look, same splendid swing."

If the Civil War curtailed Angel's career at one end, a deficient childhood diet and an excitable temperament shortened it with stomach ulcers at the other. Nonetheless, by the time he had effectively retired, in his mid-40s, Angel had won three tournaments in Britain, two Spanish Opens, come fourth in the 1957 Open at St. Andrews and played five times in the US Masters. Perhaps most importantly, he won the individual World Cup (then the Canada Cup) in 1958.

If Angel Miguel was putting Spain on the golf map by his World Cup win, however faintly, a much more significant event was taking place in Madrid that same year. At Club de Campo, the second most esteemed club in the capital city, a school was built for caddies. It was a neat, modest building, tucked out of sight below the pro shop. Metal-working benches occupied the concrete floors

and, on the wall, a cast-iron plaque advised the boys in the ways of a good caddie. "Golf", it concluded, "is your principal means of life."

The sentiment of the plaque, if not exact replicas, was to reappear in caddie schools up and down the country. In little over a decade there were about fifteen such schools, all attached to and run by wealthy clubs and all based on the Campo project. Boys enter the schools at eleven years of age, study manual crafts such as metal-work, and are made available to caddy for club members throughout the day. It is a unique school system, hardly egalitarian by instinct (Spanish caddies, however impressive, are never selected to representative amateur teams), but one which, almost incidental to its purpose, has become a breeding ground for professional golfers. It played a major role in lifting Spain into the upper levels of world golf.

The Miguel brothers were to extend the fame of Spain in the sport. The less stylish Sebastian, the more dependable player, partnered by Seve's uncle, Ramon Sota, led Spain in a thrilling challenge in the Canada Cup played in 1963 in Paris. They were beaten on the final hole by Palmer and Nicklaus. Sota accepted the defeat as inevitable. "The Americans are invincible," he said while his partner, Sebastian, posed for a photograph with Nicklaus. "You will not find me in the picture," Sebastian then told a friend. "I am too little." It took a long while – fifteen years, and the arrival of Seve – to instil self-assurance among the Spaniards.

Sota, then 27, became the next leading Spanish golfer. A bulky, fierce player, Sota was a paradoxical one: inelegant but efficient, slow to play his strokes but so eager he often ran between shots, quiet yet so highly strung that he habitually tossed blades of grass into the air to judge winds that didn't exist. "Palmer hitches up his trousers," he would say. "My habit is to toss grass."

In his blunt way Sota may well have been the best player ever produced by Spain, prior to his nephew. He won the Open championships of Spain, Portugal, Holland, Italy and Brazil. He scored a 62 in one round at St. Nom-la-Breteche, to triumph in the 1965

Augusta National, 1980. 15th hole, last day, the Masters. Seve's crucial second shot carried 285 yards over the lake and on to the green to ensure victory. By winning at Augusta Ballesteros replaced Jack Nicklaus as the youngest man ever to have won two major golf championships.

7

Royal Waterloo, Belgium, 1976. 2nd hole, last day, Swaelens Trophy. From a cluster of trees Seve punched a 5-iron through a gap in the branches – into the hole for an eagle 2 and certain victory over Gary Player.

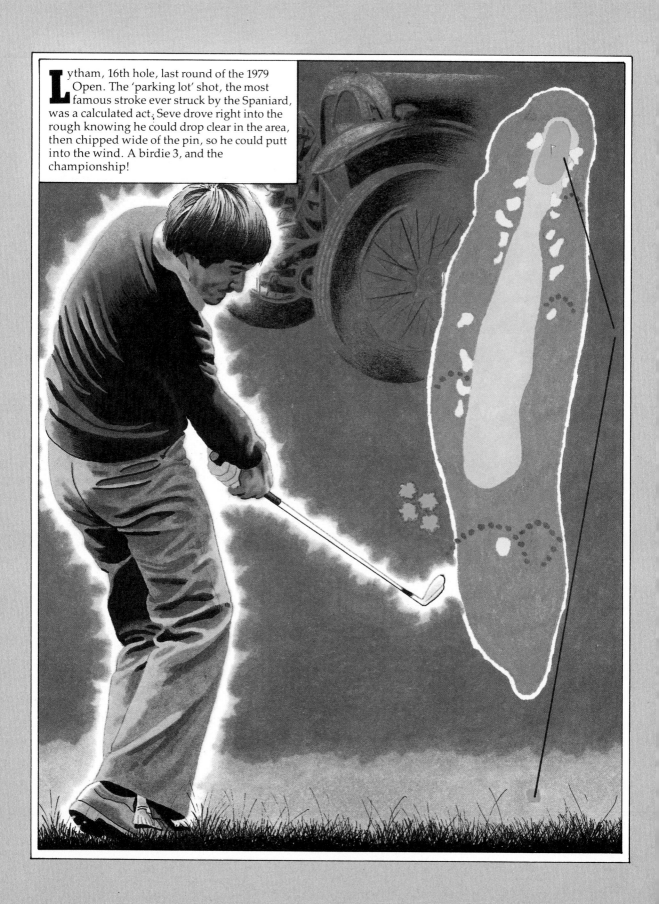

Lytham, 16th hole, last round of the 1979 Open. The 'parking lot' shot, the most famous stroke ever struck by the Spaniard, was a calculated act; Seve drove right into the rough knowing he could drop clear in the area, then chipped wide of the pin, so he could putt into the wind. A birdie 3, and the championship!

French Open with an awesome 268 total. He also finished sixth that year in the US Masters, the lowest Continental finish until Ballesteros's victory.

The period between Sota and Ballesteros and the caddy-school graduates was bridged by the Madrid player, Valentin Barrios, Ballesteros's brother, Manuel, and by Angel Gallardo, from Sitges near Barcelona. Barrios was probably the best golfer of the three but rarely left the Continent. Gallardo and later Manuel Ballesteros did more than any other Spaniards of their day to keep Spain on the international scene, playing in Latin America and often alone among their countrymen on the British tour.

It was in the late 1960s that the impact of the caddie schools was first felt when German (pronounced, 'Herman') Garrido, a former student at the school at Campo, won the inaugural Madrid Open of 1968. Garrido was to be followed by his elder brother, Antonio, and by Manuel Piñero, all of the Club de Campa, and by Jose-Maria Canizares of Puerto de Hierro and the breath-taking Salvador Balbuena of Malaga, an exquisite striker of the ball who died of a heart attack on the eve of the French Open in the spring of 1979.

It was against this background that Ballesteros returned to Spain a fortnight after his Masters victory to play in the Madrid Open. He does not like playing in front of his home crowd. "People in Spain feel I must win every time I play, as though I am a football team, and this makes the pressure worse," he says. He adds, "Also, I don't like it when people cheer me. I like it better when they cheer against me." A familiar refrain.

In Spain, Ballesteros's international record had been comparatively poor. His best run at a big title on home ground came in 1978 when, after squandering an early lead, he finished third in the Madrid Open, also at Puerta de Hierro. Ballesteros feels, as do many other Spanish professionals from humble backgrounds, that he is exploited by the Royal Spanish Federation of Golf, the game's Establishment in his country, who do little to bring golf to a wider public. He is also scornful of the Spanish press. "You only give golf any importance when I win," he snapped in an acrimonious *El Pais* interview which took place the week following his Madrid Open victory. "When I win everybody says he was my friend years ago – and it's not true."

The 1980 Madrid Open was to be the most momentous golfing event in Spain's history. From the start it was a fiesta. The entire Ballesteros family came down from the North, along with a coach filled with villagers and driven by Ramon Sota. Madrid itself appeared slowly to have awakened to the joys of golf, for gallery ropes were brought in to restrain the crowds that were to surge up and down the hills.

Ballesteros appeared at the course on the first practice day to discover that his regular European caddy, Dave Musgrove, was engaged for the season by an English player, Mike King. Musgrove, who had not heard from Ballesteros throughout the winter, would not change bags. In the uneasy atmosphere it was finally decided that Baldomero should carry his brother's clubs.

Puerta de Hierro, which in 1962 was reconstructed by the English golf architect John Harris, is a hilly course which rises and plunges tightly between Umbrella pines and olive trees and around one big, bald hill. The length is 6,932 yards, the par 72. Ballesteros opened with a solid 68, which left him a stroke behind Piñero and set the stage for a remarkable two-man battle for the crown. Of the second day Peter Ryde of the London *Times* wrote: "In spite of a firm intention to find someone else to write about in the Madrid Open golf championship, except Severiano Ballesteros, the Spaniard made it impossible again today to switch attention from him."

The reason for Ryde's continuing interest in Ballesteros was the Spaniard's astonishing score on the second day: a 63 which, according to Seve himself, was not only the lowest championship score he had ever returned but a round that matched anything he played at Augusta or Royal Lytham in his big championship victories. He played in suppressed, dark fury, mumbling all the while to his

Spanish golfers Antonio Garrido (*left*), with whom Ballesteros won the World Cup in 1977, and the tragic Salvador Balbuera, considered by many to be the most stylish of all Spanish players. The likeable Balbuena, who died on the eve of the 1979 French Open, had for weeks been forecasting his own death (by heart attack, it turned out) to his family and friends.

caddy-brother: "I will have another birdie here . . . I can win every tournament in the world." When King Juan Carlos was pointed out in the gallery, Seve didn't look up; in fact, it wasn't until after his round that he realised Royalty had witnessed his record. When Seve missed an eight-foot putt on the ninth green, giving him only a par for the hole, Baldomero comforted him by saying he made the turn six under par, a 30. Ballesteros snapped back: "It should have been a 29."

Into the unknown: Seve's brother, Manuel, at Sandwich, England. He led the way for his brother on the world tour, sacrificing his own potentially rich career to advise and look after the promising youngster.

Still in a dark cloud, he returned with a 33, this time missing a 6-foot putt on the home hole for what would have been his *tenth* birdie of the day. Still, the resulting 63 was nearly faultless, a course record, and it gave Ballesteros a three-stroke overall lead over Piñero. The highest tribute, however, was that fellow pros Brian Barnes and Mike King went out on the course to watch their great contemporary. "Nobody in the world plays like Seve," says Barnes. Piñero scored a 69; Ballesteros led the rest of the field by five strokes.

After the third round the two Spaniards were out by themselves. Piñero returned a 69, Ballesteros a 70: Seve's lead was cut to four. Paired on the last day, the two drew the largest crowd ever to watch golf in their country: whistling, shouting, bustling fans, many of whom had never before seen the game. Piñero, who had won the Open in Madrid on the same course, put up a battle. By the end of the fifteenth he had drawn to within a shot. At this point one of the hidden subplots so common to golf unwound. Piñero's caddy, Jimmy Cousins, was hobbling with a sore foot. He chose to go on ahead, down the fairway, rather than attend the 16th tee with his man. "I should have gone back with him," Cousins says now. "He needed me; I let him down."

The sixteenth, a 394 uphill par 4, is a tempting hole, with danger lying in the Umbrella pines to the left of the fairway. Piñero, first to drive, was rigid with excitement. His caddy watched in agony from a distance as he saw the little Spaniard address the ball and quickly lurch into his shot. Under tension, golfers tend to hook, and so it was: the ball soared up the hill and suddenly veered towards the trees. "If I had been with him," says Cousins, "I'd have calmed him down." Then Ballesteros, with the road open, followed Piñero deep into the pines. Galleries broke loose, sweeping up the fairway. Surveying his brother's desperate lie, Baldomero's face went ashen with fear. Seve laughed. "Don't worry," he said, wholly relaxed. "I love playing these shots." And so he did: an astonishing 7-iron shot bent sharply out and round the trees, some 125 yards, the

ball finishing just six feet from the hole; an eventual birdie 3.

Piñero, chopping out of the trees as any mortal might do, was forced to settle for a bogie 5. That was to be the difference: Ballesteros 69–270, a remarkable eighteen strokes under par, with Piñero 70–273. Fans stampeded round Seve. Ballesteros had won an international event for the first time in Spain. After the ceremonies his family, some dozen strong, and with wives and children, were given an upstairs room in the clubhouse where they dined and celebrated the victory. Later that evening Ballesteros and his exhausted brother/caddy, Baldomero, went out on the town with a couple of friends. Seve later told the story:

"Baldomero is a very nervous person and not used to carrying a golf bag that weighs 20 kilos [44 pounds] up and down hills for four days. Eight kilometres a day for a man 33 years old made him very tired. His nervousness, plus the pressure, plus all the eating and alcohol and the smoke and the excitement . . . We were on a street in Madrid much later, and Baldomero just fall down. On the pavement. He stops breathing."

Their two friends, a couple, fell weeping into each others' arms. Seve, also fearing his brother dead, dropped to his knees to give him the kiss of life. But Baldomero revived and was taken to the hospital for observation. He was released as dawn came over the city. "*Que susto!*" recalls Seve. "What a scare!"

Sadly, the classic struggle between Ballesteros and Piñero may have been the high point in the history of Spanish golf. Ironically, a glance through the teeming crowd, upwards of 6,000 that followed that final match gives an inkling of the problem. Among the most informed were a scattering of the nation's top young amateurs, well dressed and prosperous, but members of a social class which considers itself above the hurly-burly of professional golf.

Also in the gallery were some two dozen of Spain's teaching professionals. They are bright, qualified mentors who have eschewed the tournament circuit in favour of comfortable careers giving instructions to wealthy club members and multitudes of tourists. In Spain the teaching of golf is a vast and growing business: at the exclusive Puerta de Hierro club, in fact, there are 17 teaching professionals, a number that would be hard to surpass anywhere in the world.

As to the fate of the tournament pro in Spain, consider Ballesteros and Piñero, the two principal protagonists at Madrid. Ballesteros is a 'one-off', outside the mainstream of Spanish golf, and beyond catagorizing. Piñero, on the other hand, arose from the wellspring of the Spanish professional game, the caddy school system. And this wellspring is drying up: one after another, the caddy schools are shutting down.

"Spain is changing socially and economically," says Piñero. "Club members now use trollies, so there is not enough work for the boys in the schools. Also, the standard of living is going up. Fathers prefer to put their boys in schools where there is more opportunity to train for a good job." He shrugs and smiles as he thinks of the consequences of all this. "It is good for Spain, but bad for Spanish golf. After our generation I think it will be a long while before you see any more good Spanish professionals."

Driving

The two most important clubs in my bag are the driver and the putter because, deep down, it is good for my confidence to start a hole well and finish it well. I sometimes use a driver as little as a half dozen times a day but, of course, it is psychologically important to hit a good drive. To do this, you first must remember two basic things we already have discussed, rhythm and clubhead speed.

Rhythm and clubhead speed are more important in driving than in any other golf shot. When you have good rhythm, and you want to hit a really long drive, you don't swing fast. It is not the answer. Instead, you make a longer swing, take the hands a bit further back. You slow down the swing, backswing and downswing, but you speed up the hands through impact. That is all.

Let me tell you the two fundamental problems I have had over the years with my driving and maybe you will benefit by my explaining how I have tried to solve them. Since I was a boy, trying to hit balls as far as my brothers, almost all my power came from my right hand. I would guess that 80 per cent of it came from my right and 20 per cent from my left which, most probably, is more than any other successful professional.

In the first few inches of my takeaway I moved the clubhead straight back with my right hand which gave a wider arc and a longer, more powerful swing. But it cost me much accuracy because my right shoulder would also go 'up' and my right elbow 'out' automatically. This 'flying right elbow', which also used to be noticeable in Jack Nicklaus's drive, resulted in an inconsistent swing and less accurate shot. Nicklaus has improved that flying elbow, at the cost of driving distance, and as I practised for the 1980 Masters I decided to do the same thing. It has been partially successful and I am still working on the orthodox swing which follows. I suggest you use it:

Start the backswing with both hands with the left shoulder, left hip and left knee all moving together. With that start to the backswing the right shoulder does not, or should not, go 'up', and there should be no flying right elbow. The right shoulder should go round rather than up. This may not give such a powerful swing but it can give a more consistent one.

My second problem has been my position at the top of my backswing. My swing is so full that in fact sometimes I overswing, so that I can be pointing with the club not at the target but to the right of the target. Obviously, I lose accuracy with this swing. Now I try to adjust a little; go a tiny bit 'inside' in starting the backswing instead of straight back, so as to make my swing a little bit flatter. I find that my club will point more at the target at the top of my swing.

Once you have your rhythm and swing under control, you are ready to work on the two basic drives which you need for your game. One is the power drive, a slight draw which for me can reach 300 yards, and the other, just as important, the slight fade of about 260 yards with no roll. The first, of course, is more dangerous and demands a safe, open landing area whereas the second, played down tight fairways, still gives you greater length than a 3-wood or iron off the tee.

The long ball: The key to this drive lies in the address. Tee up the ball higher than usual and stand slightly farther away from it in a slightly wider stance. The ball, a couple of inches farther forward than normal, should be about opposite your left instep. Your grip will now be slightly longer up the shaft. All these little adjustments will give you a flatter swing, one that has to move in an inside-out plane, and the result will be the slight draw you are looking for.

Then relax. Your muscles must be loose to get the maximum turn and club speed you need for this long ball. On the takeaway, brush the grass. The backswing is low and on a wide arc, with the body moving laterally to the right. Keep the right leg braced, and if there is a pulling in your neck rotate your head slightly to the right. When your club is about halfway back, about 45 degrees above the horizontal, your shoulders will have nearly completed their turn, your hips just beginning to turn. You now have established your 'long bull' swing, so proceed as normal, always remembering to keep the swing full and long and, of course, accelerate on impact.

The Drive: set-up, take-away, impact and follow-through

CHAPTER NINE

BACK CHAT

"If you want the greatest possible amount of gratuitous and well-meant advice, you should have something the matter with your knee or, failing that, your back."
Bernard Darwin, *Playing the Like*, 1934

The cynicism of Darwin, the late and esteemed golfing correspondent of *The Times* of London, is shared by Ballesteros. "I don't trust doctors," he once told me. "They are like golfers. Every one has a different answer to your problem."

If there is nothing the matter with Ballesteros's knees (although don't give him the chance to speculate on it), there certainly has been trouble in his back. Like many golfers, he complains of pains at the base of his spine and, like most, he entertains only a vague suspicion of its origin. Basically, it may be structural, for there is something wrong with his frame. A layman can see that plainly: the Spaniard's right shoulder, as we saw in the locker room at Royal Lytham, drops below the left. This would suggest either a fault in the shoulder or, less noticeably, a lateral curvature of the spine, a hiking over – a scoliosis, in medical terms.

So far, so good, but such are the complexities of back complaints that even the interested layman can raise other questions. Is the source of Seve's tilt hereditary or environmental: that is, is it inherited or acquired through the surroundings of his lifetime? A single piece of evidence supports either notion: Seve's eldest brother, Baldomero, walks with a similar tilt. On the one hand, that suggests a family trait; on the other, it may simply be good evidence that each carried heavy bags over their right shoulders as caddies!

It is interesting to note that this right-hand dangle, whatever its cause, has probably had a salutary effect on the Spaniard's game. The British writer Christopher Plumridge, writing in the London *Guardian*, illustrated it amusingly in an article entitled "Ballesteros is out on a Limb". He tells of having dinner with the Spaniard and asking him, "How do you manage to hit the ball so far?"

Ballesteros stood up from the table and demonstrated how: his right finger tip hung far below his left. "The discovery of that physical phenomenon allowed everything to fall into place," wrote Plumridge. "While you and I when addressing the golf ball have to drop our right shoulder to place the right hand in the correct position on the grip and also check that, in so doing, we have not pointed our shoulders left of the target, Ballesteros can get into the correct address position by virtue of a natural defect." Plumridge might have added that Ballesteros's further-extended right arm might also allow him a fuller follow-through.

Anyway, Ballesteros at least can remember the incident that may initially have brought the injury. He also can remember vividly when his back first bothered him as a golfer. It came at the age of 14 when boxing. His opponent accidentally stepped on his foot. Ballesteros, pulling away, fell on his coccyx. The pain was fairly lasting: "I was for two weeks limping," he recalls. He recalls, too, straining his back in lifting rocks as a boy on the family farm.

It was on the day prior to his first professional tournament, which in itself is perhaps significant. Burning to triumph in the Spanish PGA's Under-25s tournament, that year held at his home course of Pedrena, Ballesteros hit 700 practice balls and the next morning awoke with pains snatching at his back. The weather, which had been chill and wet on practice day, continued, and Ballesteros was

forced to play his first round of competitive professional golf with the aid of pain-killing injections. He scored a 68 and won the tournament with ease. The year was 1974 and he was 16 years old. The chill and strain of that long-ago practice day almost certainly was the cause of his later back trouble.

The troubles continued and early in 1977 Ballesteros, at the behest of the Spanish Golf Federation and especially his friend Ceballos, saw an eminent Madrid orthopaedic surgeon, Dr. R. Carbajosa. Resisting, the Spaniard underwent a series of X-rays which revealed small vertebrae damage, particularly low in the back, especially in the fifth vertebrae, which links the spine to the base of the back.

"His injury was not severe," Dr. Carbajosa later recalled, "but if not treated it not only could be painful but also could develop unfavourably and stop him from playing golf as a professional." He suggested Seve rest for six months from the game and sleep with a board under a hard mattress: common and sensitive palliatives.

Ballesteros tried the board, rejected the rest. Besides, he had been talking with another famous back sufferer, Lee Trevino, and literally, like a bolt from the blue, he all at once had reason to worry about his back. Ballesteros had been struck by lightning during the 1976 Scandinavian Open championship in Sweden, a light but frightening blow. A similar accident, much more severe and terrifying, had befallen Trevino. It came vividly to their minds.

Golf's most famous bad back in recent times has been Lee Trevino's. His signature swing, the thigh-slide that finishes locked against the left hip, had for years nagged at a childhood lifting injury. However, it took a freak accident in the summer of 1975 to do the crippling damage. It happened during a storm at the Butler National Golf Club near Chicago when, in the Western Open, a bolt of lightning struck a lake on the course, raced across the wet grass and slammed into

Trevino and his partner, Jerry Heard. "It sounded like somebody hitting a couple of hammers together: a high-pitched whine, louder and louder," Trevino later recalled. "I started shaking, my heart stopped and I couldn't breathe. Then I passed out and lay there, suspended above the ground."

Trevino suffered shock, burns on the back and this curious sense of levitation – but, following a brief stay in hospital, he rejoined the tour. He felt perfectly fit until, six months later, he heard a 'knuckle-crack' while working in his El Paso garden. His back began to trouble him. He hobbled through the 1976 season, passing up the Open championship at Birkdale. At the end of the year he entered hospital in Houston for a complete check-up by eminent Spanish-born orthopaedic surgeon, Dr. Antonio Moure.

Needles 'this big' were used to test Trevino's nervous system and finally a miogram was taken. A dye was put down his spinal column and the course it took was played against a screen. Trevino watched. "Well, the fluid never got down to my tail-bone," Trevino was later to explain. "It suddenly laid up short and sort of bulbed out between the fourth and fifth lumbar vertebrae. That meant the disc was ruptured at that point. The surgeon took it out and promised I would be back at work, full time, and I believed him. He's a Spaniard." In time, Trevino indeed was back at work. Well, any friend of Trevino's – and a Spaniard into the bargain – was worth consulting, and in 1977 Ballesteros saw Trevino's surgeon in Houston, Texas. A discal hernia was noted. He was advised to undergo an operation to fuse his damaged vertebrae. Ballesteros refused, protesting that, at best, it would alter his swing and, at worst, he feared he would be a cripple.

This diagnosis brought on a terrible emotional set-back for the Spaniard. If anything, he began to attack the ball with more fury than ever: in effect he felt he had better gather his rosebuds while he could.

By 1977 his back pains began ruining his sleep and bringing on tortured dreams. The lack of sleep clearly affects him. "Sometimes I

Lee Trevino, hit by lightning in 1975 (inset) in special protective hat some months later. He believes the injury contributed to his continuing back problem.

wake up and my head doesn't feel right," he once told Michael McDonnell of the London *Daily Mail*. "My eyes are strange. I know I will not play well. My eyes are not sharp. I look at the green. I have to ask my caddy how far it is."

He turned to fringe medicine, most notably acupuncture, first under Japanese practitioners, later under a Chinese, "Mister King," back in Santander. As late as the spring of 1982, playing in a domestic tournament in Madrid, he actually was wearing hair-fine needles, covered by tiny bits of sticky-plaster, behind his right knee and in his right shoulder. He wore them less out of necessity than habit.

The Spaniard visited eye specialists, wondering if this new ailment was linked to his back. It wasn't. His throat and nose came more validly into question, for he coughs a lot, especially when striding with a frown on his face after an errant golf shot. An American eye-ear-nose-throat specialist cleared all these organs of complicity in his back problem but his nose-throat malady was real enough. Upper nasal constrictions were causing the Spaniard to breathe through his mouth, drying out his throat and causing him to cough: Ballesteros underwent surgery on his nose late in 1980 and was again to do so before the 1982 season. But by then his back was on the road to recovery.

He was getting real if temporary relief from his "Gravity Gym," that trapeze device he had discovered at the home of Graham Marsh, in Western Australia, in the autumn of 1979. Three times a day, most notably before his triumph in the 1980 Masters, he was dangling, twisting and lifting himself to strengthen his back muscles. Physically, this was the most important factor in Ballesteros's subsequent recovery. Psychologically, there was one hurdle to surmount: he needed medical assurance that he was not doomed to permanent injury by the nagging back.

That assurance came on 1 December, 1980. At Ed Barner's request, Ballesteros stopped off in California on his way back to Spain from Japan. He was taken to an orthopaedic surgeon in Long Beach, California.

The surgeon examined the Spaniard extensively. His report stated that Ballesteros's pupils were equal and reacted to light, his mucous membranes were normal, as were his reflexes, sensations and muscular functions. In short, there was nothing wrong with his nervous system; he was neurologically sound.

The surgeon then put the aching Spaniard under an X-ray. The hip joints were normal. The lumbar spine was X-rayed and found virtually normally. "There is," reported the surgeon, "a slight narrowing of the fifth lumbar interspace" – that is, some lower disc damage but nothing worth surgery. There was evidence of some Scheuerman's Condition involving the upper lumbar spine, especially of the second lumbar, which could have accounted for Seve's habit of neck-twisting. Scheuerman's Condition is a deformation of the vertebrae during adolescence, often rounding the shoulders; but sufferers grow out of the affliction.

Ballesteros was also given widespread tests for arthritis and for *ankylosing spondylitis*, a mysterious, frightening and irreversible disease which progressively stiffens the spine.

The surgeon prescribed a course of Naprosyn, an anti-inflammatory drug, and sent the Spaniard on his way. He then wrote a report to Barner. "He has widespread aches and pains, but no neurological changes, and nothing apparent of an organic nature," he said. "I really find relatively little wrong with the young man. He is very tense, which could contribute to his troubles." Ballesteros months later remembers the doctor's comments, almost *verbatim*, and clearly they put his mind and back at rest. "The doctor said I was under too much tension," he recalled and then, for the first time in his professional career, he said, "I don't worry about my back any more."

Ow! Ballesteros's back rarely bothers him more than it did during the 1979 Open, as shown here on the 13th tee on the last day.

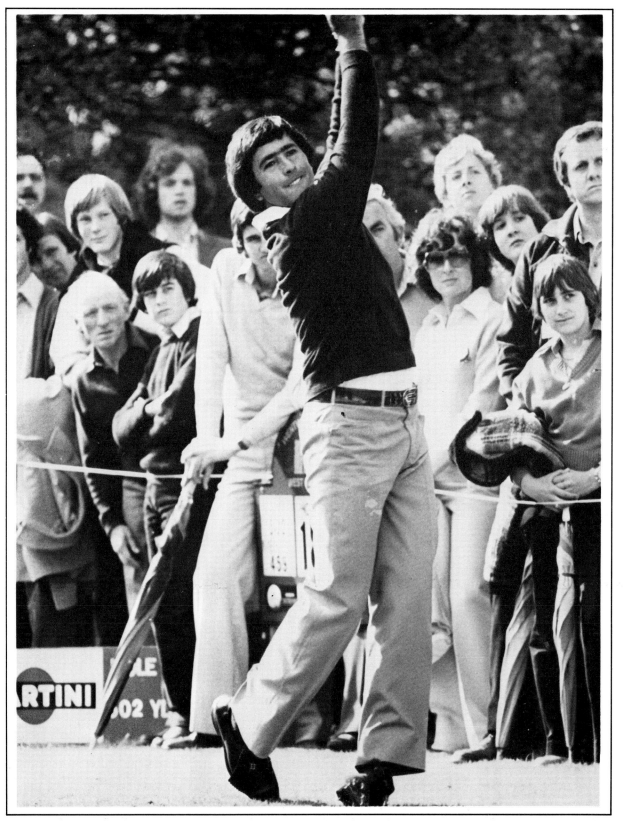

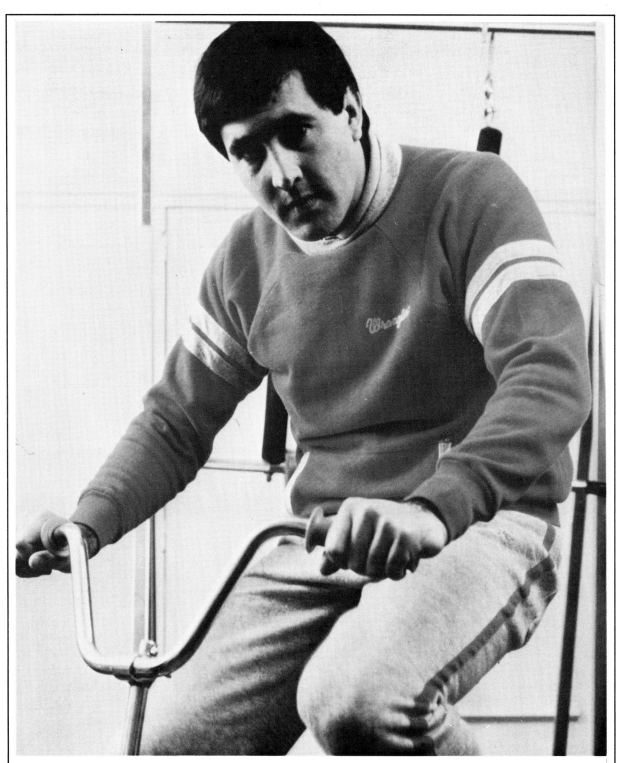

Pedal power: Seve got relief, and built up his back muscles, by exercising on the stationary bicycle at his home in Pedreña.

Trouble Shots

In my clinics I always hit a few trick shots, like the one-legged bunker shot pictured earlier; I'm making a joke, sure, but I can play it because I am good at trouble shots. Why? Because I've had lots of practice playing them, in and out of tournaments.

It is impossible, of course, to give many instructions on how to play trouble shots. Every one presents a different problem. So, my first piece of advice is to practise them. Try playing an entire round from trees and rough, as I did as a boy. Choose all the wrong clubs, too, and play them out of the craziest places: from the long irons to the short irons, even chip out of rough with a driver. The results will not only be a better understanding of trouble shots but, technically, it is good for your swing. Playing from the rough gives you power in the wrists and hands and trains you in moving your hands quicker in getting your clubhead through the ball.

Also, and this is important, practising recovery shots improves your confidence and concentration.

Here are some basic tips:

The rough: My general rule is to take a club much more open-faced than the distance calls for; that is, if the distance suggests a 4-iron, play a 6-iron because, remember, you must get the ball *up* out of the rough. If the grass is with you, that is, lying over in the direction of the green, maybe go in this case with a 7-iron.

Remember, too, that your ball will tend to come out of the rough in the direction the grass lies. Therefore, if it lies from left to right, you must aim a little bit left of your target and, in the same way, if it lies from right to left, aim slightly right.

Finally, your swing from the rough. *Very important*: your takeaway in a shot from the rough should be very, very slow. The faster you take away, the less distance you will get. What I do is to make believe I'm fishing with a fisherman's fly-rod. I take the club back slowly, like a fly-rod, then I *whip* it down,

snapping my wrists through the ball on impact.

Trees: It is very difficult to give tips about playing from the trees because every problem is different, but I find that unless your path to freedom is obviously a low hook or slice, always look for a high escape route. If you are faced with a shot that must go low, under a tree, take a long iron – the 1, 2 or 3 – position the ball more towards your right foot, grip down the club, keep the hands forward at the address, take a short backswing and, again, keep the hands forward at impact. The ball will stay low.

In conclusion, get into these habits on trouble shots: 1) don't take foolish risks; 2) study the percentage of success you might have with the shot; and 3) be positive. Also, of course, *practise* trouble shots. As you will have read in Chapter 7, I practised very much from the trees at home in Pedrena before I won the Masters at Augusta in 1980.

Rough treatment: whip through, as if the club were a fishing rod

CHAPTER TEN

LATE TO TEE

"Severiano Ballesteros takes the rough with the smooth. Just like his Rolex."

Magazine advertisement

On the morning of 6 June, 1980, a wide-bodied Iberia jetliner flew westward from Madrid towards New York. Ballesteros sat in economy class, first row, centre section, with his necktie loose and his legs stretched out. In his lap lay a small leather bag. He tilted back his head, closed his eyes and once again the name of the greatest golfers in his lifetime went through his mind: Bobby Jones, Jack Nicklaus, Sam Snead, Ben Hogan, Arnold Palmer, Lee Trevino. . . . These men had won at least two major championships in succession – the press had made Ballesteros vividly aware of this over the past several weeks – and now he himself was after his second major title in a row. He was on his way to the US Open championship at Baltusrol, New Jersey.

The Spaniard was not happy. "I'm worried about my chest and my throat," he said, frowning. "I'm taking antibiotics and I'm very *flojo*, weak." He considered the implications of what he had said. "When you are weak, you lose your rhythm."

From across the aisle his brother, Baldomero, looked up from the Madrid morning newspaper he was reading. "Bob Shearer had a 63 in the first round of the Atlanta Classic," he said. The news pleased Seve. He liked the Australian. Also it was good to hear that someone who played often on the European circuit was beating the Americans. "Nicklaus scored a 78," added Baldomero.

The Nicklaus news surprised Ballesteros. It noticeably – and I thought, as I sat beside him, unduly – puzzled him. The Spaniard was taken aback, not so much by the poor score, although that was not to be expected from such a fine player so near to the US Open, but by the fact that Nicklaus was playing in the Atlanta Classic at all. "What's he doing there?" asked Seve. "Why isn't he practising at Baltusrol?" Ballesteros had come to expect that Nicklaus, the meticulous preparer, would spend the week before a major championship practising at the site. Now Nicklaus's approach appeared to throw into question Seve's own decision to practise at Baltusrol.

Baltusrol. The Spaniard enjoyed a brief moment of fun trying to get the proper pronunciation of the peculiar place name, taken from a certain Mr. Baltus Roll, a farmer who once owned the land. Baal-*too*-strall, he tried. Baal-to-*strall*. The alien golf course grew large and menacing in his mind. Ballesteros went suddenly solemn, considering not the place-name but the challenges of the course. "Are the greens big?" he asked me.

It seemed an odd question. Yes, all US Open greens were big.

"I like small greens. Small greens mean that good chippers will have the advantage. I believe I am one of the best chippers in the world," said Seve ". . . Are there many trees?"

Baltusrol was no jungle, I replied, but, yes again, there were trees. Ballesteros turned this over in his mind. "I have learned one thing in the last year and that is that you cannot attack a course if you are in the trees," he said. "In practice I will drive the ball short."

Ballesteros's mind then retreated into its own private forest, a place impenetrable, indeed dangerous to others. After a time he opened the lumpy bag on his lap and took out a medicine bottle. From it he shook two pills. "These are vitamins for the brain," he said. "I can't stop my brain thinking. Lately I have been thinking very much about my future. I will retire when I am ready, maybe when I am 40. But I wonder, what will I do when I retire? I would like to have a nice job, no pressure, no autographs, just a place to go alone and sit down."

The Spaniard swallowed the vitamins dry. He replaced the bottle in the bag which contained an assortment of other medicine bottles. There were pills for his heavy cold, pills for his chronically bad back, sleeping pills and countless vitamins and herbal potions. Ballesteros then idly leafed through an in-flight magazine which carried an article on himself, *El Campéon*, but he genuinely is embarrassed by celebrations of his own glory. After a cursory glance he put the magazine aside. He coughed. He shifted in his seat to settle his back and stared towards the window.

It was at that point, or perhaps at a later moment in the journey, that Ballesteros afterwards contended that a dark premonition passed through his head. "In the airplane," he recalls, "I remember saying to myself: 'Seve, you should not be going to the US Open. Something bad is going to happen.'"

The Spaniard was right. Something bad did happen.

In retrospect, Ballesteros's journey to Baltusrol seems doomed from the start. The first evening passed pleasantly enough. We walked round the small city of Summit, New Jersey, site of Baltusrol. Ballesteros went to bed early and Baldomero stayed up, chatting about his brother's childhood, clearly nervous at the prospect of the championship. The following morning we travelled by courtesy car, those private cars laid on by the home club and driven by lady members, to Baltusrol. It was an impressive sight: massive clubhouse, endless buggies, rolling lawns.

Things began to go wrong on that first practice day. Ballesteros registered in the clubhouse and was given his appropriate badges. One badge gave him, as a player, entrance to the dining room. Seve requested another for his brother. The United States Golf Association official, while friendly, was firm: caddies were not allowed beyond the locker area. Ballesteros argued. The official held his ground and the Spaniard, feeling his brother was being snubbed, stalked angrily to the locker room.

Hale Irwin was there, changing his shoes. Irwin was not only the holder of the US Open title but, the previous summer at Lytham, had played that final round of the Open championship with the Spaniard. The two men in the past had been notably unfriendly towards each other but Irwin asked Seve to join him in a practice round; Ballesteros accepted.

Ballesteros played beautifully and drew a huge following of club members. He also played with foresight, testing places he might meet in the championship. He was rarely wild off the tee and, by the loosest of measurements, was many strokes under par for the day. He had lunch in the clubhouse while Baldomero was secreted into the Press dining tent by British journalists. On subsequent practice days, Marin ate with the journalists.

In all, Seve appeared ready for the battle. On the eve of the first round, however, Seve had an argument with his manager, Ed Barner. Barner said the Spaniard should attend a Rolex cocktail party in New York City, some twenty miles away, because he was about to sign a contract with the watch firm. Ballesteros refused; he had a championship to play the following day. Barner persisted, pointing out that a car was laid on for the Spaniard; he need not stay long. Ballesteros held his ground; he remained at the hotel.

He might just as well have stayed there the following day. In the first round of the championship, paired with Irwin and Mark O'Meara, the US Amateur champion, Ballesteros played wretchedly. He missed fairways one after another, and putts slid away on the greens. The Spaniard returned a 75, five strokes over par. Seve was bewildered. "I cannot remember a day when I don't score at least one birdie."

Seve's score left him joint-85th, a precarious position since only the top 60 would survive the second day. It was also a dozen

strokes behind the leaders, Nicklaus and Tom Weiskopf. These two veterans had both scored 63, which was not only a new course record but tied the single-round record for the championship that Johnny Miller set in the final round when he won in 1973 at Oakmont, Pennsylvania.

If the Spaniard's prospects looked bleak they were not totally without hope for he had made up such deficits in the past. Further, he had no history of ducking gunfire, and at breakfast the following morning he appeared relaxed and cheerful. Barner had flown off on a business trip to Brazil, leaving his colleague, Joe Collet, to look after the Spaniard. It had been Collet who so carefully reminded the Spaniard of his starting times each day at the Open championship at Lytham. Tragically he did not do so on the second day at Baltusrol.

At 9.25 that morning, Ballesteros set out for the club with his brother. Their tournament chauffeur, the lady club member, later recalled that the brothers were chatting and joking the whole way and made no comments about the heavy traffic that clogged the streets. As Ballesteros climbed from his car in the car park at the course, a British journalist shouted that he was due on the tee. The Spaniard sprinted to the locker room, hurriedly pulled on his spikes, and rushed to the first tee. It was too late – by seven minutes. Irwin and O'Meara were moving towards the green. Ballesteros protested. The starter, John Laupheimer, a respected USGA official, had no choice but to disqualify him under Rule 37-5 of the Rules of Golf. It reads:

> Time and Order of Starting
> The player shall start at the time and in the order arranged by the Committee.
> Penalty for Breach of Rule 37-5: *disqualification*.

Strictly speaking, there is no provision for leniency under this Rule, but much to the displeasure of the Royal and Ancient Golf Club of St. Andrews, the game's ruling body

Disqualified from the 1980 US Open Championship at Baltusrol, Ballesteros leaves his hotel for the airport.

Looking for luck: Seve, an animal lover, tried
vainly to get back on track, as he did here in the
European Open, after his damaging blunder at
Baltusrol.

outside the United States, the USGA is willing to allow a player to start with a two-stroke penalty if his partners have not yet played their second shots. This loophole was closed: Irwin and O'Meara had both done so; at the moment, they were putting on the far-distant green. No other extenuating circumstance could be found for Ballesteros's tardiness. The disqualification stood.

The Spaniard exploded in fury. The penalty, he said, was too severe. He blamed the traffic; players should have their route cleared to the course. He said he never again would play in America and, collecting his shoes from the locker-room, returned to his hotel. There he refused to open his door to newsmen. Inside, with myself and Collet, his fury was too intense, too continuous to have been assumed. If he had wilfully missed his starting time, the act had been subconscious.

Ballesteros soon issued a statement: "I thought my tee time was 10.45 and so I left my hotel at 9.25. The trip took us longer than usual because of the traffic. It took about 20 minutes. I arrived three-four minutes late. I was very hot when I heard the decision and that's the reason I left quickly. I didn't want to say anything there I'd be sorry for. I am very disappointed, but that's all the facts." With that, the Spaniard flew back to Madrid the same evening, Friday the 13th, and by late the following night was home, practising, at Pedreña.

Ballesteros might well have survived the midway cut, for a second round of 71 for a two-round 146 total would have seen him into the top 60 players. As it was, after the second day Nicklaus appeared to be running away with the championship. His 71, following his 63, gave him a midway championship record of 134, two strokes clear of the Japanese Isao Aoki and three lesser-known players. As Seve skulked in distant Pedreña, Nicklaus continued his assault. After a 70 in the third round he stood on 204, six under par, joint leader with Aoki, who returned his third successive 68. On the final day, paired with the Japanese, as he had been throughout the championship, Nicklaus took command early; apart from a fleeting moment midway,

the great American led from start to finish. A final birdie putt and Nicklaus was home in 68. His 72-hole total of 272 smashed by three strokes the championship record he had set at Baltusrol in 1967, the year he unseated Palmer as king.

Not until Wednesday, nearly three full days after the result was known, did the Spaniard acknowledge an interest in the result. A Scottish golf writer, Alister Nichol of the *Edinburgh Evening News*, travelled to Pedreña to carry out a pre-arranged interview. Nichol tactfully mentioned that since Seve hadn't won it at least it was nice that Nicklaus had. "Nicklaus won?" Seve said, looking up from a practice shot. "How did Aoki do?"

Ballesteros's wound was to fester long and deep. It was discussed widely throughout and after the championship. P. J. Boatwright, the USGA president, could not remember a player being disqualified from a major tournament for being late to the first tee "in the last twenty years", and Nicklaus himself said evenly, "I usually try to get out here an hour beforehand." It also stirred memories of other major disqualifications in the recent history of the game.

The most ludicrous took place in the 1940 US Open at Canterbury Golf Club, Cleveland, Ohio, when six players, all experienced Americans, were disqualified. In those days two rounds, 36 holes in all, were played in threesomes on the final day, and at lunch on this occasion Edward (Porky) Oliver and Ernest (Dutch) Harrison were well placed with the afternoon round to play. A storm threatened, however, and Oliver was eager to get going before it broke. He was wrongly advised to set out 'provisionally', pending a ruling. "I was having lunch," recalls Joe Dey, then director of the USGA, "and they just took off – even though the course manager tried to restrain them."

Oliver, Harrison and their partner, Johnny Bulla, went out 28 minutes early. The

Beauty and the Beach: Ballesteros, who courts no regular girlfriend, spent weeks at home in Pedreña during his troublesome summer of 1981.

following threesome of Ky Lafoon, Leland (Duke) Gibson and Claud Harmon also set out before their assigned starting time. The players were disqualified, as was Ballesteros, under Rule 37-5. The decision was especially painful for Oliver, a perennial runner-up in tournaments, for his score that afternoon, a 71, would have qualified him for an 18-hole playoff for the title.

In 1957, disqualification from a major championship also struck the Hawaiian Jackie Pung. She had comfortably won the US Women's Open championship at Winged Foot, near New York, when it was discovered that her last round card, certified for accuracy by her signature, contained a lower number for one hole. It was of little comfort to her that the club members took up a collection that outstripped the first prize she had lost.

Mrs. Pung's disqualification came under Rule 38-5, which reads:

NO ALTERATION OF SCORES
No alternation may be made on a card after the competitor has returned it to the Committee.
If the competitor returns a score for any hole lower than actually taken *he shall be disqualified.*
A score higher than actually taken must stand as returned.

It was the last sentence of the Rule, the 'must stand' one, that brought about the most famous and heart-breaking rules incident in the history of the game. The occasion was the 1968 Masters. The principals in the drama were the Americans Bob Goalby and Tommy Aaron and Seve's friend and mentor, Roberto de Vicenzo. On the final day, which was also de Vicenzo's 45th birthday, he and Goalby came out of the pack to challenge for the title on the closing holes. De Vicenzo birdied the 17th hole with a 3 to take the lead, then dropped a shot with a bogie 5 on the 18th for a glorious 65. Goalby, playing just as splendidly, cruised home later with a 66. Both totalled 277 for the tournament and it appeared they would playoff on the following day.

As the two left the roped-off scoring area,

de Vicenzo's playing partner and 'marker' for the day, Aaron, glanced at the Argentinian's card. Something was wrong. Its total was 66 and, worse, Aaron had erroneously entered a par '4' instead of a birdie '3' on the 17th. Worse still, in the confusion and excitement of the moment de Vicenzo had signed the card, certifying the score. De Vicenzo was called back; he acknowledged his fatal mistake. It was not the wrong '66' that undid him, for only incorrect scores for individual holes are punishable under the rules. It was the awful '4'.

The rules committee pondered the problem and, frankly seeking a loophole that would allow the Argentinian to playoff for the title, they visited Bobby Jones, the founder of the Masters, in his cottage near the tenth tee. Together, the men considered reinterpretations of the rule. None could be found and Jones confirmed the sad truth: de Vicenzo's higher score stood. While not disqualified, he dropped to second place, a single stroke behind Goalby. "I look over the card three-four times and all I see is the 5 for the 18th," de Vicenzo said later. "In the pressure I lose my brain. I play golf for thirty years all over the world and now all I can think of is what a stupid I am to be wrong in this wonderful tournament."

The affair was discussed for weeks that season with players sharing pity for de Vicenzo, Goalby and the blundering Aaron. "Twenty-five million people saw Roberto birdie the 17th hole," said the respected veteran Jimmy Demaret. "I think it would hold up in court." Others stuck by the letter of the law. "No matter what you say," said Arnold Palmer, "it always comes back to Roberto." For himself, de Vicenzo made no complaints.

The event was made all the more poignant for having taken place on the Argentinian's 45th birthday, the sunset of his career. The normally sedate Augusta galleries had sung "Happy Birthday to You" as he passed down the fairways. De Vicenzo never again challenged seriously for a major title.

Years later, considering Ballesteros and the 1980 US Open, de Vicenzo looked on

the Spaniard's disqualification as a mixed blessing. "It was bad, but maybe it was a nice thing, too," the Argentinian said. "Some days you have to make a mistake and, you know, you then have a new way to make a victory."

Victories were sparse in 1980; in fact, the Spaniard's sole win came late in July when he triumphed over a weak field in the Dutch Open at Hilversum. Publicly Ballesteros stood his ground, mulishly refusing to acknowledge his error at Baltusrol. "I always put the fault to somebody else," remained his credo, on the course as well as off. The USGA were to blame, or the traffic.

Privately, though, he admitted to the flaw that so worried his friends. "I am very unstable," he confessed. "Many times I get more disturbed by people than I should." People that most disturbed him that summer came in fantasies. "Many times I see people, at night. Not in dreams. . . . No, no. I tell you, *people*. I wake up and see a body leaning over my bed – maybe a man, maybe a woman, I don't know – but when I open up the light, nothing. It has gone away."

That particular dream – or, as Ballesteros would have it, incident – was only one of many. All of them were relevant to unpleasant experiences he had suffered in golf. In one he was blindfolded and was facing a firing squad but woke in the nick of time. In a second, playing in a World Cup with his countryman, Piñero, he failed to hear the summons to the first tee and was disqualified. In a third, he won the US Open championship, then woke up and, *poof*, the trophy had disappeared from his uplifted hands.

Throughout 1981 the Baltusrol incident was never far from the surface. Nor, to Seve's credit, was his gallows humour. Once, on a practice green late in October, I noticed a massive, golden Rolex Oyster Day-Date watch on his wrist. Ballesteros, in turn, noticed me looking at it. He tapped the watch twice, brutally. "Nice watch, eh?" he said. "I must always wear it. It tells me the time I must tee off." His smile was weighted with anger and, as it remained frozen, not a little challenge. If anyone was to poke fun at his Baltusrol blunder it would be he alone, Ballesteros.

Keys to the Game

Before my Masters triumph I prepared for weeks at home, putting on the hard beach and shaping my shots high and right-to-left down the tree-lined fairways of Pedrena. But during the four rounds at Augusta I had only one thought in mind, one 'key': *Seve, start back your swing in one piece*. I was thinking of this all the time, nothing else, and I played very well.

That was my key for the Masters. It lasted me for about three months, during which I scored two victories in Europe. Then suddenly it no longer worked. Somehow it no longer 'fitted' my swing. The 'key' didn't open the door to success and I spent the rest of the summer looking for another. I found them, like 'first take the club back, *then* turn,' or 'keep the legs still.'

While playing golf, you see, I must have a key in mind, something to concentrate on when playing a shot. In fact, I sometimes carry a bunch of keys in my mind: one for the woods, another for the irons, a third for bunker shots, and so on. But I use only *one* key for each shot which, I am told, is what the great Bobby Jones thought. He used to say that he played best when he had only one thought in mind, not so good when he had two thoughts and badly when he had more than two thoughts. That is the way I feel too.

It may seem strange that one key may work for months – or even for only a day – and then suddenly no longer fits your game. This is because I have different feelings at different times and you must fit in with what you are feeling at a particular time. Also, a key may stop working because you are becoming too aware of it, exaggerating it and spoiling your swing. Or, as I say, your feelings may become different. I am sure this is true with all golfers.

Reminders: Bobby Jones had a key to the game

CHAPTER ELEVEN

PEDRENA REVISITED

"The tragedy of 1981 has been the virtual eclipse of Severiano Ballesteros . . . He belongs to yesterday and nothing is duller than old news."

Louis T. Stanley in his annual *Pelham Golf Year* (1981)

"Severiano Ballesteros . . . the Best Golfer in the World." Annual world rankings.

Golf World March, 1982

The course of a golfer's career, like true love, never does run smooth. Technically, physically and mentally the promising young player is tested and, unless made of the soundest of stuff, found wanting. Ballesteros underwent such tests. First, technically, it was thought through the early years, chiefly after he came to public notice with his fine run at the 1976 Birkdale Open, that his 'flying elbow' would bring him to grief. Then, physically, his bad back raised doubts, not least in his own mind, that his talent would never reach fruition.

In 1980 and 1981 those critics sceptical of the Spaniard's rapid progress felt they were finally rewarded. The Spaniard, they decided, had fatal character defects: he could not stand the pressure of greatness and, more unattractive, he was seen to be greedy and ungrateful to a game that had lifted him out of pigs-in-the-basement peasantry.

Writing in the *New Yorker* after Seve was disqualified from the 1980 US Open at Baltusrol, Herbert Warren Wind expressed this notion with caution and charity. "There seems to be a streak of capriciousness in Ballesteros," he wrote. "Almost as though he had risen to stardom too suddenly and had trouble adjusting to the realities of the world."

Wind was right. Ballesteros did have trouble adjusting. The Spaniard *was* capricious – was, literally, as the Oxford Dictionary has it, "guided by whim, inconsistent,

irregular, incalculable." In short, Ballesteros was as complex a young champion in 1981 as he had been a fledgling professional back in 1976.

It was in the middle of this testing period – in February 1981, when he was still shell-shocked by his tee-time blunder at Baltusrol and still to be battered by the battle with the European Players' Tournament Division over appearance money – that I visited him in Pedreña. It was five years since I had last seen him in the family's stone farmhouse and while, on one level, the differences were enormous, on another they could not be noticed. His surroundings had changed but Ballesteros, although deeply troubled, was the same young man.

About a quarter of a mile south of the old farmhouse, on the last little hill of the village, stood the Ballesteros's new home. It is a two-storey villa, solid and unfussy, with lawns back and front and a pair of gables peering from the red tile roof. The family had been in the house for only a few months. A smell of cement lingered, and on the front lawn a seedling still wore its identity tag. The weather was cold and changeable – a burst of sunshine one minute, drumbeats of sleet the next – but the villa was centrally-heated and warm.

In the commodious kitchen, Seve's mother looked lost among her sparkling chrome sinks and chocolate-brown cooking units. She was dressed in a flowery silk dress and her hair was done up in a springy new permanent wave for, that evening at the golf club, Seve was being honoured with full social privileges – nearly a year after winning his second major championship. The señora admitted she preferred the old farmhouse. So had Blaster, she said. The family dog had gone missing, never to return.

Seve's voice, followed by telephone silences, could be heard from down the hall in the living room. It is a big room, with a picture window, an Afghan carpet on the parquet floor. On the walls hung a map of Royal Lytham and St. Annes, site of Seve's 1979 Open victory, and a framed letter of congratulations on winning the 1980 Masters from Jimmy Carter, written on White House stationery. On the television stood an autographed photograph of Spain's King Juan Carlos.

The three trophy cases stood against the far wall. In them were three Spanish Gold Medals of Merit for Sport, the actual Masters' Green Jacket on a hanger, cups, clocks, statuettes and a trophy, a small replica of the Open championship trophy, which called to mind a strange and interesting story Ed Barner once told.

"Over the years I've tried to show Seve my appreciation for what he's done by giving him nice things," said Barner. "I had a book of his press clippings bound in leather and, during a tournament, I had it sent up to his room. He never said 'thank you' – never even acknowledged it. Another time, after he had won the British Open, we had a replica of the trophy made up by Garrard's, the silversmiths. My wife and I took it to Spain and had a terrible time getting it through customs. When we got to Pedreña Seve was pleased enough to get it. He showed it to his mother. Again, no reaction. No thanks. I couldn't understand it at the time, but I do now. Those gifts, the leather-bound book and the trophy, embarrassed him. They also took away his initiative. He likes most to give things to people. He'd rather give than receive – but, either way, he has to do it on his own terms."

Seve was stretched out on a modern sofa, speaking through a red telephone. He was dressed in a red track suit trimmed in grey, and bright white training shoes. The family's new black-and-white kitten, Sookie, lay curled on his lap. The colours made a stunning composition: black, white, grey and, of course, the red telephone. It looked all too studied: a setting for *House and Home* or the London *Observer*'s colour series,

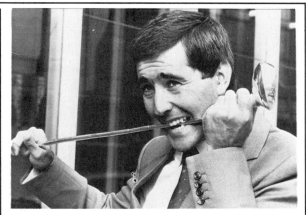

Ballesteros poses with a silver golf club, the symbol of the La Manga, at what was to become a memorable press reception in February of 1981 in London.

A Room of One's Own.

Ballesteros is aware of this celebrity image and, as though to mock himself and the furniture of fame that surrounds him he emits an emphatic little sigh of fatigue. It was a conspiratorial gesture, meant for me. *Isn't this ridiculous*, it said, *Don't believe what you see.* When Seve rang off – he had been talking, or rather listening, to a Cuban representative of his American clubmaker – he stared at the telephone for a long while then suddenly his mood darkened. He looked drained, world-weary. "Every day, business and rain, business and rain," he said. "I have no time to *think*. I have no time to relax, to concentrate on practising my game. I tell you, never have I been so poorly prepared for a season. I will play no good at the Masters."

Straightening, Ballesteros winced and, reaching behind himself, pulled out a padded frame he had been using to ease his discomfort on airplanes. From under his sweat shirt he pulled a hot-water bottle which had been placed there to soothe his 'aching' ribs. "Maybe one of these days there will be a big surprise when people open up their newspapers and read the headline, 'Seve Ballesteros Retires'."

To what? Seve's absorption in golf is worrying. He is keenly aware of what Trevino once told him: "If you don't take up a hobby pretty soon, you're gonna drive yourself crazy." Why didn't he take a long hunting holiday – as Watson and Weiskopf did – and get away from it all?

"Trevino and you and everybody have suggestions for me," he fired back. "I don't know if I should have a holiday. I don't know if I should have a girlfriend." When it comes to women, the Spaniard is susceptible, although decidedly male chauvinist: in a now infamous interview in the Madrid newspaper, *El Pais*, he told a woman writer, "You women want equality, but you'll never get it because women are inferior to men in all sorts of ways – physically, intellectually, and morally. There are exceptions, but on the whole women are inferior to men."

All of a sudden, Ballesteros glimpsed something through the picture window. He jumped up, spilling Sookie on to the carpet. He tossed the hot-water bottle aside, dashed to the hall closet, pulled out a .22 calibre repeating rifle, opened the front door and sank into a kneeling position on the steps. *Pow! Pow-pow-pow!* Crows lifted heavily from a far tree and flapped low towards the distant mountains. *Pow-pow.* The racketing sound echoed up and down the valley and died. Ballesteros rose and, remembering his aching back, winced again before returning empty-handed to his villa.

Seve occasionally hunts rabbit in the mountains and shoots duck on the River Cubas but his reason to bear firearms extends beyond sport. When in 1981 the Spanish footballer Quini was kidnapped Seve, who lives near Basque country, applied for and quickly received (as did his father) permission to own a .38 calibre revolver for protection.

Ballesteros was troubled by more than his back, his ribs or, indeed, fear of imminent abduction. He foresaw the storm which would inevitably break over his claim for appearance money from sponsors of British and Continental tournaments that season. He would weather the storm, but not before much costly damage was done to his professional and personal reputation. His money troubles were to be the off-course golf story of 1981.

Appearance money is nothing new. As far back as Willie Morris, and surely farther, golfers have been paid to appear in competition. In the 1960s and 1970s Mark McCormack brought it to a fine art, first with Arnold Palmer and later with Tony Jacklin. After Jacklin's victories in the 1969 US Open and 1970 Open, McCormack charged £2,000 for him to appear in European tournaments and £10,000 in Japanese ones. In Europe, this was done with the approval, even encouragement, of the then-Tournament Players' Division adviser John Jacobs, who was trying to build a healthy tour.

It served its purpose. The tour, with Jacklin the star performer, grew and flourished. All parties were happily rewarded as long as Jacklin's form held. It didn't. By the mid-seventies he began to falter. Sponsors began to pay him in instalments: £1,000 to show up, the other £1,000 if he finished the tournament. Appearance money began to fall out of favour among sponsors and envious players. In 1976, the newly-formed European Tournament Players' Division of the (British) Professional Golfers' Association formalized and expanded the rule: hereafter, the only ETPD members who could request appearance money were those who had either won any of the three major titles (for these purposes, the US PGA was not considered a major event) or had finished the previous season as leader of the British Order of Merit.

With their policy (or lack of one) towards overseas players, the ETPD left a door open to future troubles. Any overseas player, at least if he was not a member of the ETPD, was allowed to demand any amount of appearance inducement to play in Europe. There was, of course, no legal or moral way to stop this practice; and besides it was considered a fine thing: such famous players as Trevino, Weiskopf, Miller and Crenshaw, and occasionally Nicklaus and Watson, beefed up live attendance and television interest by their presence at a golf event. In any case, the number of their appearances was limited by the willingness of PGA Tour officials in America to release them from conflicting home tournaments.

However, these fees angered players

who felt the game would be better served if the monies were spread through the tournament prize lists. And Ballesteros didn't help matters by remarking, "I think some of my fellow professionals are jealous of me."

It was against this background that in the autumn of 1980 the ETPD – led by chairman Neil Coles and vice-chairman Angel Gallardo – took a decision. Hereafter no ETPD member could request appearance money apart from 'expenses' of $10,000. "Our first loyalty has got to be to the system," said Ken Schofield, secretary of the ETPD, with an eye to the weaker sponsors, "not to the individual player." The overseas players, of course, would continue their $30,000–$40,000 raids into Europe.

It was after this decision that Barner and Collet made a fundamental, if understandable, misjudgement: they thought it wouldn't stick. They believed sponsors would ignore the decision and, as long as not actually bidden, offer even sweeter fees than the $20,000-plus Ballesteros commanded and received in 1980. Also – although Barner especially did not want to play this old game – there was the charade whereby the Spaniard could be paid under the table or say, by appearing at a cocktail party or 'jumping over a rope' for a 'fee' of $25,000 on the eve of the tournament. "And, at the last resort, there was the law," Collet said later. "We thought the rule was not only unfair but illegal; if necessary, we could beat it in the courts." UMI maintained their truculent, doomed stance with the sponsors: 'take it or leave it'.

Barner and Collet had not reckoned on the tenacity and persuasive powers of Schofield. In the first few weeks of 1981 Schofield marshalled the sponsors into a common front, partly through threatening to force his member golfers to boycott any tournament that broke the rule. The one sponsor to defy Schofield publicly was John Spurling of the Bob Hope British Classic; but in the public's eye even that was turned to Schofield's advantage, for the Classic was partly organized by and was a 'poodle' to Barner's UNI-Managers International.

As the storm brewed, Barner, Collet and

Ballesteros felt they had British and European public opinion on their side. It would have been, indeed should have been, if the Spaniard had been better briefed on how to court this sympathy. Instead, Ballesteros blundered into a hail of bad publicity. Two incidents in particular turned the public against him.

First, on 11 February, Ballesteros appeared in London to sign a five-year contract with European Ferries. He would be tournament professional at their La Manga club in Spain. The press conference was called chiefly for property and travel writers, but the golf writers came too and raised the question of appearance money. "Sponsors don't have to pay me appearance money," Ballesteros said ingenuously, "but also I don't have to play in their tournaments. I think it should be left to the sponsors to decide who they want and how much they want them. If sponsors want all the publicity then they must pay the good players."

He added that he planned to play six times during the season in Japan. "Over there they play for double the prize money and they are prepared to pay me a much better appearance fee," he said, "It can be as much as $30,000–$40,000 for one tournament." Seve then posed for photographers by biting down hard on the shaft of a solid silver golf club – the hand that fed him, so to speak, and the emblem of La Manga. The image con-

Unhappy threesome: Ballesteros with Neil Coles and Jose-Maria Canazares, two colleagues who opposed his inclusion in the Ryder Cup team.

veyed in the British press the following day was not flattering. Ballesteros, for his part, was hurt by the reports: 'some friends', the British Press who were not only savaging him on his side of the Atlantic but spoiling his name with similar articles in influential American golf magazines. Ballesteros's 'money-grubbing', together with his Baltusrol 'walk-out' did him severe, although not lasting, damage in the United States.

Second, on 5 April, four days before Ballesteros opened his defence of the Masters title, London Weekend Television put out a television documentary, *Brian Moore meets Seve Ballesteros*. It was a lifeless piece of film mostly because Ballesteros, although paid £10,000 for his co-operation, felt the camera crew was intruding on his private life. He was preoccupied with worries over the appearance money squabble, moreover, when the last film footage was shot in February in Pedreña. One exchange he had with Moore, subsequently watched by thousands in Britain, probably did more damage to his image than either his disqualification from the 1980 US Open championship or the forthcoming dispute with the ETPD. The relevant passage went:

BM: May I put a point to you then, that I think a lot of people will be saying at this moment, that golf has given you a lot, maybe you should give golf something back by not requiring appearance money?
SB: Do you know how much I give to golf? I start since I was 9, and since then I live until I am now 23, that way all for golf, you think that is not enough? I think that is enough.
BM: Your life?
SB: My life, and the life is more important than anything else, right, so golf owes me something, or maybe – but I don't owe anything to golf. You agree with that?
BM: I agree with that. How do you feel finally on the money side? If appearance money were abolished how would you react to that?
SB: What do you mean?
BM: If appearance money was ruled out.
SB: Appearance money will never disappear.

Will never disappear. How can you – let me explain to you, how can you bring Hale Irwin, Tom Watson, Lee Trevino from America to play any tournament in Europe if they have three times more prize money in America – how will they come to play in Europe and fly 10-15 hours? It's understandable, you think, eh?

It doesn't take a close study of the passage to suggest that no jury would convict Ballesteros of avarice on its evidence. True, the Spaniard's black glower during the exchange couldn't endear him to viewers, but his honesty could not be denied: I have worked hard at golf, he was saying, and I deserve the rewards I have reaped. It was a view that cut across the Corinthian ethic of British sport and, rightly, Ballesteros was later baffled by the hostility it inspired. How different it would sound if we heard: I have worked hard at medicine (or bricklaying), and I deserve my rewards.

Ballesteros, meanwhile, had received a stern letter to his home from Schofield. "One thing you should know straight from me," wrote the ETPD secretary. "Is that *no one player* can, from this day forward, expect to clear $250,000 in appearance fees before teeing off on the European Tour."

Anyway, there can be no doubt that through the season Seve duly suffered for his part in the appearance money battle. It weighed heavily on his mind at Augusta the week of the television documentary and his forecasts for 1981, which had been delivered on the sofa in his living room, came true with dispiriting accuracy. He played 'no good' at the Masters. He opened with a wretched 78, added a lacklustre 75 and, by a gap of six strokes, failed to qualify for the final two days of play. It was the first time the Spaniard had missed a Masters cut and, more humiliatingly, he was the first holder to do so since Jack Nicklaus in 1967 – at least comforting company.

It was to be the beginning of a dismal season of major championships for the Spaniard. In June, in the depths of despond, he came joint 41st at the US Open at Merion. "I didn't talk to anybody that week," he recalls, "because they would remind me of my starting time at Baltusrol." In July, he was never in the hunt for the Open title at Sandwich and, in August, he narrowly missed disqualification from the US PGA championship at Atlanta when he showed up on the first tee in the nick of time on the second day. "If I was late again," he remembers wryly, "I was planning to say I was sick and had come to pick up my clubs and go home."

Trouble meanwhile had been bubbling along on the home front. After his disaster at the US Masters, Ballesteros declined to defend his Madrid Open title or to play in the Italian Open the following week. He secured the required releases from the organizers of these tournaments and announced that he would be playing in two others in Japan. Anticipating (rightly), that the ETPD would not release him to compete in these conflicting tournaments, he resigned from the body. "It is, we feel, a necessary provisional measure to safeguard him against any possible disciplinary action," said Collet, who mailed the resignation from Los Angeles. "If he is not a member this week, he cannot be breaking any rules."

Such Catch-22 cynicism could hardly be applauded and Ballesteros's stock among his fellow players dropped further a fortnight later when, paid a full appearance fee of some $25,000, he played in the French Open at Paris. What if he were fined by the ETPD for playing in Japan, he was asked on the eve of the championship? "If it is £5 or £500 I will not pay it," he said, "What happens after that, I don't know." What happened after that – apart from the Spaniard playing nicely to finish joint-3rd in the championship – was that his resignation was accepted 'with regret' the following week by his peers in the ETPD committee.

Ballesteros was therefore out of the running for a place in the Ryder Cup team which was due to play the US in the autumn at Walton Heath. He would also be restricted to three tournaments on the European circuit. This suited the Spaniard who felt even more wounded and done down. "I felt everybody was against me and I became scared of

people," Seve recalls. "I felt like I was in a restaurant, alone, and people whom I didn't know were talking about me."

As the battle waged between Wilshire Boulevard and the ETPD offices at Wentworth, Ballesteros spent the summer in exhibition matches, those hapless sorties to the United States and mostly practising long hours in Pedreña. Once, he ventured out for a tournament, the Scandinavian Open at Linkoping – for the full $25,000 appearance fee – and won it, putting like a genius. Seve shrugged off the victory. "*Destino*," he said, although it was due him. "It was just destiny."

The Scandinavians had paid the full appearance fee, as had the French, because their contracts to do so had been signed before the ETPD ruling forbade them. Ballesteros now had no tournaments, apart from the Open the following fortnight, on the near horizon. Pressure for a settlement was piling up: Bernard Langer was now in control of the European circuit, a dour substitute for the glamorous Spaniard. Slazengers, club- and clothesmakers to Ballesteros, were preparing to press their 'disincentive' clauses in any new contract with the truant Spaniard.

As for Seve, he began to realize there was nowhere but in Europe for him to exercise his art. "I was using up my exemptions in the United States and I couldn't keep flying back and forth to Japan," he said later, "and at home the ETPD, right or wrong, were making the rules. I was growing older. What could I do? I must play golf."

On 11 August, in a release issued from his manager's office in Los Angeles, Ballesteros formally reinstated himself into the ETPD. In the statement, Barner pointed out the fine results by Europeans in the Open (Langer came second, while four other Europeans made the top ten) and indicated that in future the ETPD tournaments might not need

---

Close encounter: Ballesteros and the companionable Ben Crenshaw were head-to-head through most of the 1981 Suntory World Matchplay championship before the Spaniard won on the last green.

the extra drawing power of American professionals. "This could signal the end of guarantees," he said, "and a dramatic rise in prize money on the ETPD tour."

Ken Schofield, while making no specific reference to guarantees or appearance money, welcomed back the prodigal son. "We feel," said Schofield, "the problems encountered over our conflicting events will not recur." Wounded vanities had been soothed all round and, best of all, Ballesteros was back in the fold, eager to play golf.

And back he came, to take vengeance for the injuries, real or imagined, that had been dealt him. In the remaining fifteen weeks of the year – and on into the first three days of 1982 – Ballesteros was not only to return to form but to excel himself. He played in eight tournaments and won four of them, in four different countries. He came second twice and third once and, just for the statistical record, was under par in twenty-seven of the thirty-five rounds he played. It represented probably the finest extended stretch of golf in his life.

Royal Liverpool, at Hoylake, was his point of re-entry. The tournament was the European Open and Seve received no appearance money other than the approved $10,000 'expenses' for travel and hotel bills. Inactivity had dulled the Spaniard's competitive edge and, while putting together splendid rounds of 68-68-67 on the opening days for a four-stroke lead he came unstuck under the finishing pressure applied by his playing partner, Graham Marsh. He soared to a 74 and lost by a pair of strokes to the Australian. The next week, in the Tournament Players' Championship at Dalmahoy, he needed a 63 on the last day to join a playoff, which Brian Barnes won over Brian Waites, but missed it with a 64. A fortnight after that, in a tournament which, ironically, would pay appearance money to Ballesteros, he made no impact, finishing far behind the winner, Langer, in the Bob Hope British Classic.

The 1981 Spanish Open was held at El Prat, a gently undulating course, amply scattered with Umbrella trees and built on seaside wasteland near Barcelona. Its big holes are for big hitters; indeed three of the five par 5s stretch more than 550 yards. Clearly, if Ballesteros stayed out of the trees and if the seasonal wet wind, the *garbi*, stayed quiet the layout would suit him.

Still, in April Seve had chosen to play in Japan rather than defend his Madrid Open title, and among the Spanish press and the Spanish golfing establishment he sensed an air of hostility. He was tense; his forearms actually bulged as he swung his clubs in practice. "I was putting too much pressure on myself because I wanted to win so much," he recalls. "I was not relaxed. I was afraid to hit the ball and follow through." He scored an opening 71, six strokes adrift of the leader, Sam Torrance, then a 67, which drew him to within four strokes of the new pacemaker, the Argentine Vicente Fernandez.

It was Ballesteros's putter, if any club, that was letting him down, and on the third day the Spaniard had reached the third green when, waiting for his partner to play, he stood at the fringe and idly practised his putting stroke. Suddenly a notion struck him: the stroke was wrong. "On the takeaway I had been lifting the left wrist, which was opening the face of the blade," he recalls. "I found that if I cocked the wrists downwards a little on the take-away the putter stayed square to the ball."

He returned a 70 and lost ground. He was now five strokes and five men behind the pacemakers, Fernandez and Spain's Canizares, who stood on 203.

The Scot Steve Martin and the Zimbabwian Tony Johnstone were on 206 and the Englishman Bill Longmuir on 207. Ballesteros fancied his chances. Martin, Johnstone and Longmuir were not proven class players. As for the leaders, they seemed more like three rather than five strokes ahead of him. Seve's basis for this idea: "Canizares is not a good front-runner, especially in front of Spanish people. He doesn't like pressure. And Vicente just isn't long enough for the par 5s. Also, they will be playing together. They will fight each other and forget about me."

Ballesteros was prepared to cope with

these rivals. What he didn't fancy, looking ahead, was a 1981 season that droned on through Britain, Australia, Japan and South Africa. On the eve of the last round in Barcelona, he took a decision. "I'm not travelling to Australia and the Far East," he told Collet that night. "I'm not mentally prepared. Cancel my entries." Only after much argument with Collet, brother Manuel and Ceballos did he relent.

The final day was fine and without wind; Ballesteros was relaxed. On the practice area he told a huge gallery, the cream of Catalonian sporting society, that he would play *'en broma'* – for the fun of it. He added, for the record, to television: "It looks like everything is arranged. A 65 will win us the championship." And he returned to his old feeling, "Destiny is on our side."

Destiny – and thousands of fans – were indeed on Seve's side. Canizares and Fernandez fell away, as did the other front runners, save Martin. Ballesteros, however, was too much for the Scot. The Spaniard defeated the long holes, "stole shots," as he put it, "over here, over there, like a gypsy," and with his new self-tip putted as he had not done since his purple patch in 1976. He duly returned a 65, as though on order, to win the championship by a single stroke over Martin. It was one of the last titles he most sought, his own national Open.

The Suntory World Match-play championship, played the following week at Wentworth, was another title that had eluded Ballesteros, and he came to England in a high, useful pique: the championship officials had insulted him. He had been the last man invited. The field showed its customary gaps: Nicklaus declined his invitation remarking that October was a good month to watch his son play football and, besides, he was too old for 36 holes in a day. Watson also declined, pleading a previously-planned tour of Japan.

So the lineup read: 1981 Open winners Bill Rogers (British) and David Graham (US); Americans Hale Irwin and Raymond Floyd; Isao Aoki, the finest golfer in Japanese history, (who had won the Match-play once); the evergreen Gary Player (who had won it *five*

times); the leader of the British Order of Merit, Bernhard Langer; and two British players, Brian Barnes, who was at the top of his form, and Nick Faldo. The two late 'wild cards' were Ben Crenshaw, the popular and frequent runner-up in major championships, and Ballesteros.

Ballesteros was eager. He had never won a title in that form of play; in fact, in five times he had never even reached a Match-play final. "I should be a good man-against-man player because I like to beat people," he says, "but I'm not. Maybe in match-play I give the other man confidence. He knows I will always make a big mistake."

Ballesteros made his plans. He studied the techniques of Irwin and Player, whom he considered master match-players, and concluded that they not only made few mistakes but rarely made *big* ones. "Irwin goes par-par-par and sometimes birdie," he reasoned. "This creates much pressure. I know, I have felt it." The Spaniard decided it would be he who created the pressure. He would curb his attacking instincts, especially off the tees and, contrary to the accepted wisdom of match-play, pay attention to the course, not his opponent.

In the first round Ballesteros – of all people – drew Hale Irwin, the match-play master. Straight away Seve's caddy, Baldemero, became nervous. "It was very difficult keeping Irwin out of my mind," says Seve, "because every time he got into a bunker my brother would say, 'he can still get a par if he gets up-and-down in one.' I had to say, 'Look, Merin, forget Irwin.'"

Ballesteros, curbing his attack and scoring pars and birdies, played the best golf of the day. "Irwin expected mistakes from me," he recalls, "and when they didn't come he got impatient." From a lunchtime position of 4 up, four strokes under par, he closed out the American, 6 and 4. The next day, still playing within himself, the Spaniard brushed aside the title holder, Norman, 8 and 6. "I broke him too," Seve says, "by not making bogies."

The victory brought Ballesteros to the semi-finals, where he faced Langer. The

German is a phenomenon: he recovered from a case of the 'yips', an expression coined between the Wars by one of its sufferers, Tommy Armour. It is a putting affliction wherein the victim either freezes over the ball or involuntarily twitches in playing it. The affliction is usually terminal or, as Henry Longhurst wrote, "Once you've had 'em, you've got 'em."

Well, Langer once had 'em but he's no longer got 'em. Crippled through his early professional career by the 'disease', the German picked up an old putter in Clive Clark's pro shop at Sunningdale in 1980, liked the feel of it, bought it for £5 and miraculously recovered. In 1981, he had won two European tour tournaments, the German Open and the Bob Hope Classic, and was Europe's leading official money-winner with £95,990.

The Langer-Ballesteros confrontation was billed as the 'European title fight'. It was a needle match as Ballesteros felt, correctly, that it had been Langer's vote that had denied him a place in the Ryder Cup team. The stern German struck first, and after four holes was two clear. Ballesteros hit back, and on the short tenth hole took the lead by holing a long birdie putt. "When that happened Langer looked tense," Ballesteros remembers, "He looked like he did not expect to win." The Spaniard was right. He never yielded his lead and swept to victory, 5 and 4. Langer walked away without shaking hands, a discourtesy he later denied as intentional, claiming he had not known the score.

Meanwhile, Crenshaw was moving confidently through the lower half of the draw: he beat Faldo, 5 and 3, Graham, 5 and 3 and, in a gripping semi-final battle, his friend Rogers by one hole. The stage was set for the two 'wild card' outsiders to meet in the final.

In terms of scoring, the match was solid, unexceptional (Ballesteros was five under par for the day, Crenshaw four); as theatre, though, it was the most gripping match of the championship. Crenshaw made the early

Baldomero, Seve's brother and caddie, falls into the winner's arm on the 36th green at Wentworth.

running as he pulled three holes clear. Panic took hold of Baldomero again. "Come on, use the driver!" he implored his young brother, but each time Seve replied "No, the 1-iron. I will play the course, not the man."

Crenshaw, too, showed admirable composure, a memorable example of it coming on the afternoon tenth, that short hole where Seve had delivered Langer that early psychological *coup de grâce*. Crenshaw had let slip a lunchtime lead of two holes and now, all-square on the tenth tee, he watched in amazement – he later admitted – as the Spaniard drew a 7-iron out of his bag. The hole was 186 yards long! Yet, with a gentle sway of his hips, Ballesteros dropped the ball on the green, four feet from the flag.

Crenshaw lost the hole to a birdie but valiantly won the following two holes with birdies himself. The game continued to swing back and forth until the pair arrived, level, on the last tee. After two useful drives Crenshaw, playing first from the fairway, succumbed to the classic reflex under pressure: he hooked his approach wood wide of the green. Ballesteros played his 1-iron to the front of the green and, after Crenshaw had hit his shot well past the pin, the Spaniard ran his third stiff to the hole. When Crenshaw missed his 7-foot return putt the title belonged to Ballesteros. He and Baldomero, as they had done so often, fell weeping into each other's arms. The Match-play triumph, Seve later reckoned, was his third most important victory after the Masters and, of course, the Open.

The date was 11 October and, for most professionals, the season was over; but Ballesteros, with endorsement obligations in Australia and Japan, was soon back in action. In the first week in November he played in the Australian PGA championship at the nation's most celebrated course, Royal Melbourne. The championship coincides with another social highlight on the Australian sporting calendar, the Melbourne Cup races, which indirectly led the Spaniard to a final contretemps with the golfing establishment in 1981. The deadline for competitors to register for the championship fell on the eve of Race

Day, and Jack Newton, the irrepressible Australian, lingered long after the last race, some say in a car park with a bottle of champagne. Anyway, Newton failed to meet the registration deadline and was duly barred from the championship. Ballesteros never forgets a kind deed – Newton after all had defended him hotly, on television, during the 1980 Masters – and the Spaniard flew to his friend's defence.

The rules were ridiculous, Ballesteros argued. They should be relaxed to allow Newton to play. His appeal not only fell on deaf ears but earned him a public rebuke from Peter Thomson, once a renegade himself. "Ballesteros is a prima donna with an inflated ego," said Thomson, now established as president of the Australian PGA, "and has an exaggerated opinion of his own importance."

On the first two days it wasn't Ballesteros's ego that was inflated, it was his scoring – a 73 and a 74 – and midway through the championship he found himself nine shots behind the leader. However, he was still spoiling for a fight for the title. "If I can shoot two 67s," he announced that night at an official banquet, "I can still win this championship." Such talk, in effect, was whistling past the graveyard, for the Spaniard privately nourished little hope. He jotted off a postcard to Ceballos that evening. "I am putting like an amateur," he wrote. "I told you I never should have made the trip." On the third day the Spaniard, launching a searing attack on the formidable course, scored a 66, then a final round of 69 to win by three shots from the Australian Billy Dunk: not quite two 67s, but near enough!

Ballesteros moved on to Japan where, on greens sprayed for brighter television viewing, he won the Dunlop Phoenix tournament from a field that included Tom Watson, Langer and the best of the Japanese. "You saw him play at Lytham," recalls Howard Clark, a Briton who competed in the

T he Spaniard's claim to world golf leadership suffered a shaky passage through much of 1981 but recovered at the prize-giving ceremony following the Matchplay championship.

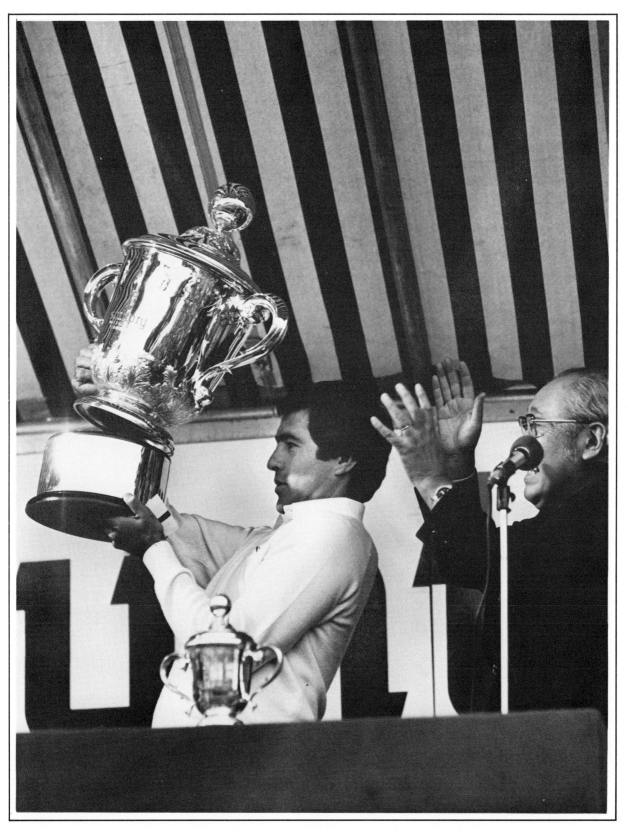

Dunlop Phoenix, "Well, he made that look quite ordinary. He was a little bit heroic." Ballesteros's heroics included improbable saves from the roughs and great banana-shaped shots from out of the trees. He won the title by three shots from Japan's Koji Nakajima.

Seve was now on a high, and he closed out the year in South Africa, competing in the controversial Sun City Million Dollar Challenge, in the tribal homeland of Bophuthatswana. The challengers were Ballesteros, Miller, Nicklaus, Trevino and, as player-promoter-designer of the course, Gary Player. It is a mammoth course, 8,000 yards long, but at 6,000 feet in altitude one that is said to play nearer to 7,200 yards.

Apart from the many moral questions raised by the extravaganza – and on this the subject and writer hold contrasting views – the competition was undoubtedly thrilling, with Ballesteros and Miller locked in one of the most extraordinary of all sudden-death playoffs – one that lasted nine holes. On the short first playoff hole Miller hit a shot to within four feet of the flag and Ballesteros, all grace under pressure, nearly holed out after him. They halved the hole. They halved the next seven, too, before Ballesteros, in gathering darkness, three-putted to lose the match.

His reputation restored as the finest golfer of his generation, Ballesteros returned home to Pedreña in the shadow of the Cantabrian Mountains and its monument raised in honour of those who had returned rich from the New World. There, on the shingle of beach and deep among the pine trees, he once again prepared for the following season. "You watch," he said, with a sense of *destino*, "I will win something big in 1982."

Putting it all Together

After each of the past chapters, I have given you tips on how to play the game, shot by shot. But golf is more than that; it is also preparation and strategy. Here, finally, are some ideas that might help you not only to play better but to win.

Fitness: For me, the best exercise is running because your legs are the foundation of your swing. All great players, such as Nicklaus, have strong legs. I try to run five miles a day during the off season, on the beach at Pedrena. Also for my legs, I lie flat on my back, spread my legs, lift my heels maybe four inches off the floor, and bring my feet together and apart, twenty-five times every morning.

My hands, I think, are the next important part of the body to exercise. I do this by stretching my hands high and clasping and unclasping, wide then tight, fifty times a day.

Before a round, I stand straight in my room, let my arms dangle down by my sides, then roll my neck and my shoulders to loosen up. I don't worry much about my diet, but I don't drink coffee.

Learning a course: I was successful in the 1979 Open because I knew in what spots I would be least penalized for making mistakes. So, when playing a practice round, stand on each tee and think: where might I get in trouble on this hole? Then play two or three shots from that place but guard against negative thinking. That is, don't talk yourself into getting into that trouble. Also, practise chipping up to the greens, close in, from all round it; this will give you a better feeling for the putting surface. Arnold Palmer practises this way.

In the practice round, think a shot ahead. Do I want to come into the green from that angle, or from another; should I leave the ball past the pin because it is better to attack it from that direction? And so on.

Tournament day practice: Play through your clubs on the practice area, as I did at Lytham, but remember always to hit a few shots at the end with the club you will use off the first tee. Make believe you are playing the same shot.

Match Play: As we saw in the last chapter, when I won the Suntory championship in 1981 at Wentworth, I had finally learned to play match-play. In this form of competition it is very important not to make bogies because if you make par, par, par, sometimes a birdie, your opponent will get impatient. It will break his concentration and, sooner or later, his game will break, too. This is what makes Gary Player and Hale Irwin two of the best match-players in the world.

Ballesteros – the complete player

FOR THE RECORD

EVENT	SITE	WINNER	BALLESTEROS	PRIZE MONEY
1 9 7 4				
INTERNATIONAL				
Italian Open	Lido, Venice	Peter Oosterhuis (GB)	5th	£1,200
Ibergolf Trophy	Las Lomas El Bosque, Madrid	Gary Player (SA)	5th	£1,440
NCR Western Province Open	Rondebasch, Cape Town, SA	Bill Brash (US)	J-8	R590
ICI Transvaal Open	Houghton, Johannesburg, SA	Vince Baker (SA)	J-12	R325
El Paraiso Open	El Paraiso, Costa del Sol, Spain	Peter Oosterhuis (GB)	J-17	£275
Beck's PGA	Wanderers, Johannesburg, SA	Dale Hayes (SA)	J-26	R230
General Motors Classic	Wedgewood Park, Port Elizabeth, SA	Gary Player (SA)	J-40	R28.75
Portuguese Open	Estoril	Brian Huggett (GB)	Failed to qualify	
Spanish Open	La Manga	Jerry Heard (US)	Failed to qualify	
Madrid Open	Puerta de Hierro	Manuel Piñero (Sp)	Failed to qualify	
French Open	Chantilly	Peter Oosterhuis (GB)	Failed to qualify	
DOMESTIC				
Spanish National Under-25 Open	Pedreña	S. Ballesteros	—	Ptas 250,000
Vizcaya Open	Neguri, Balboa	S. Ballesteros	—	Ptas 75,000
Santander Open	Pedreña	Patricio Garrido (Sp)	J-2	Ptas 15,000
San Sebastian Open	Jaizkibel	German Garrido (Sp)	2	—
Miguel Angel Gómara Open	Ulzama, Pamplona	Manuel Montes (Sp)	J-8	—
Spanish Professionals championship	San Cugart, Barcelona	Manuel Piñero (Sp)	J-20	Ptas 2,500
Cataluna Open	El Prat, Barcelona	Manuel Montes (Sp)	21	—
1 9 7 5				
INTERNATIONAL				
Lancome Trophy	St-Nom-le-Breteche	Gary Player (SA)	3	$5,000
Spanish Open	La Manga	Arnold Palmer (US)	J-6	£886
Portuguese Open	Penina, Algarve	Hal Underwood (US)	J-6	£487
Madrid Open	Lomas-Bosque, Madrid	Bob Shearer (Aus)	J-8	£438
Swiss Open	Crans-sur-Sierre	Dale Hayes (SA)	J-8	£578
Italian Open	Como	Billy Casper (US)	J-12	£428
Dutch Open	Hilversum	Hugh Baiocchi (SA)	J-15	£339
Dunlop Phoenix	Phoenix, Miyazaki	Hubert Green (US)	17	Y748,000
Double Diamond Individual	Turnberry, Scotland	Peter Dawson (GB)	J-18	£131
French Open	Le Boule	Brian Barnes (GB)	J-26	£177
Scandinavian Open	Bokskogens, Malmo, Sweden	George Burns (US)	J-26	£257
Dunlop Masters	Ganton, England	Bernard Gallacher (GB)	J-33	£110
Benson and Hedges Festival	Fulford, England	Vicente Fernandez (Arg)	J-36	£186
German Open	Zur Vahr, Bremen	Maurice Bembridge (GB)	J-41	£132
British Open	Carnoustie, Scotland	Tom Watson (US)	missed cut	
World Cup (with Angel Gallardo)	Bangkok, Thailand	US (team) Johnny Miller (US) individual	17 (Spain) 21 (individual)	No money
DOMESTIC				
Spanish National Under-25 Professional championship	Sotogrande	S. Ballesteros	—	Ptas 60,000
El Maresme Open	Llavaneras, Barcelona	German Garrido	2	Ptas 45,000
Catalunian Professional championship	Terramar, Sitges	Manuel Montes	2	Ptas 70,000
Spanish Professionals championship	La Manga	Antonio Garrido	J-8	Ptas 13,500

British Order of Merit Finish 26 (winner—Dale Hayes SA)

EVENT	SITE	WINNER	BALLESTEROS	PRIZE MONEY
1 9 7 6				
DOMESTIC				
Dutch Open	Zandvoort	Ballesteros	—	£3,931
Swaelens Memorial	Royal Waterloo, Belgium	Ballesteros	—	$7,000
Lancome Trophy	St-Nom-le-Breteche, Paris	Ballesteros	—	$17,000
World Cup (with Manuel Piñero)	Palm Springs, California	Spain	—	$1,000 (each)
British Open	Royal Birkdale, England	Johnny Miller (US)	J-2	£5,250
Scandinavian Enterprises Open	Drottningholm, Sweden	Hugh Baiocchi (SA)	3	£2,784
Swiss Open	Crans-sur-Sierre	Manuel Piñero (Sp)	3	£2,381
German Open	Frankfurt	Simon Hobday (Rhod)	3	£1,768
Portuguese Open	Quinta do Lago, Algarve	Salvador Balbuena (Sp)	5	£675
Carrolls Irish Open	Portmarnock, Dublin	Ben Crenshaw (US)	5	£1,250
Spanish Open	La Manga	Eddie Polland (GB)	J-6	£966
French Open	Le Touquet	Vincent Tshabalala (SA)	J-8	£569
Cachasel World Under-25	Evion, France	Eamonn Darcy (Ire)	J-12	£314
Is Molas Gran Primo	Sardinia	Billy Casper (US)	J-15	$1,050
Sumrie-Bournmouth tournament (with Manuel Ballesteros)	Queen's Park, England	Christy O'Connor (Ire) and Eamonn Darcy (Ire)	J-15	£97
Japan Open	Ibaragi	Kosaku Shimada (Jap)	J-16	Y762,500
Madrid Open	Puerta de Hierro	Francisco Abreu (Sp)	J-20	£220
PGA Championship (GB)	Royal St George's, England	Neil Coles (GB)	J-23	£430
Piccadilly Medal	Coventry, England	Sam Torrance (GB)	J-38	£250
Piccadilly World Match Play Championship	Wentworth, England	David Graham (Aus)	lost first round	£5,000
Lancia d'Oro	Biella, Italy	US beat Europe	halved one single, lost one fourball	$917
Double Diamond World Classic	Gleneagles, Scotland	England	won three singles, halved two single (Europe came 3rd)	£5,000
Hennessey Cup	Lille, France	Gt Britain and Ireland beat Europe	lost one foresome, won one single, lost one single	£800
DOMESTIC				
Catalunian Professionals championship	El Prat, Barcelona	Ballesteros	—	Ptas 100,000
Tenerife Professionals championship	Tenerife	Ballesteros	—	Ptas 200,000
Spanish Under-25 Professional championship	El Paraiso	Manuel Piñero	J-5	Ptas 18,000
Spanish Professionals championship	Nuevo Club de Golf, Madrid	Manuel Ballesteros	6	Ptas 30,000
British Order of Merit Finish 1				
1 9 7 7				
DOMESTIC				
Japan Open	Narashino, Chiba	Ballesteros	—	Y10,000,000
Dunlop Phoenix	Phoenix, Miyazaki	Ballesteros	—	Y12,000,000
Otago Classic	Otago, Dunedin, NZ	Ballesteros	—	NZ$7,700
Uniroyal International	Moor Park, England	Ballesteros	—	£6,000
French Open	Le Touquet	Ballesteros	—	£4,695
Swiss Open	Crans-sur-Sierre	Ballesteros	—	£7,211
World Cup (team with Antonio Garrido)	Wack Wack, Manila, Philippines	Spain	—	$1,000 (each)
Lancome Trophy	St-Nom-le-Breteche, Paris	Graham Marsh (Aus)	2	£5,143
Colgate World Match Play	Wentworth, England	Graham Marsh (Aus)	lost semi-final	£12,000

EVENT	SITE	WINNER	BALLESTEROS	PRIZE MONEY
Hassan Trophy	Royal Dar-es-Salam, Rabat	Lee Trevino (US)	3	$1,830
Scandinavian Enterprises Open	Drottningholms, Stockholm	Bob Byman (US)	3	£2,830
Spanish Open	La Manga	Bernard Gallacher (GB)	J-3	£1,736
Mexican Open	Chiluca, Mexico City	Billy Casper (US)	J-3	Ps93,300
Sun Alliance Match Play	Stoke Poges, England	Hugh Baiocchi (SA)	Lost quarter-finals	£600
Italian Open	Como	Angel Gallardo (Sp)	J-5	£967
Carrolls Irish Open	Portmarnock, Dublin	Hubert Green (US)	6	£1,400
Benson and Hedges International	Fulford, England	Antonio Garrido (Sp)	J-8	£759
World Series of Golf	Akron, Ohio	Lanny Wadkins (US)	9	$7,500
British Open	Turnberry, Scotland	Tom Watson (US)	J-15	£1,350
Penfold PGA Championship	Royal St George's, England	Manuel Piñero (Sp)	J-20	£623
Callers of Newcastle Open	Whitley Bay, England	John Fourie (SA)	J-27	£251
Skol Lager	Gleneagles, Scotland	Nick Faldo (GB)	J-31	£152
US Masters	Augusta National	Tom Watson (US)	J-33	£1,950
Madrid Open	Club de Campo, Madrid	Antonio Garrido (Sp)	J-35	£124
Double Diamond Classic	Gleneagles, Scotland	USA	won two singles, lost one singles	none

DOMESTIC

Spanish Doubles (with Manuel Ballesteros)	Escorpion, Valencia	Jose-Maria Canizares and Antonio Garrido	2	Ptas 182,000

British Order of Merit Finish 1

1 9 7 8

INTERNATIONAL

EVENT	SITE	WINNER	BALLESTEROS	PRIZE MONEY
Kenya Open	Muthaiga, Nairobi	Ballesteros	—	£4,200
Greater Greensboro Open	Greensboro, NC	Ballesteros	—	$40,000
Martini International	RAC, England	Ballesteros	—	£6,000
German Open	Cologne-Refrath, Cologne	Ballesteros	—	£6,095
Scandinavian Enterprises Open	Vasatorps, Helsingborg, Sweden	Ballesteros	—	£6,944
Swiss Open	Crans-sur-Sierre GC	Ballesteros	—	£10,697
Japan Open	Yokohama CC	Ballesteros	—	Y10,000,000
French Open	La Baule	Dale Hayes (SA)	2	£4,391
Laurent Perrier Invitational	Royal Waterloo, Belgium	Nick Faldo (GB)	2	$5,000
Carrolls Irish Open	Portmarnock, Dublin	Ken Brown (GB)	J-2	£4,687
Madrid Open	Puerta de Hierro, Madrid	Howard Clark (GB)	3	£1,356
Australian PGA	Royal Melbourne	Hale Irwin (US)	3	A$7,500
Benson and Hedges International	Fulford, England	Lee Trevino (US)	J-4	£2,312
Colgate World Match Play	Wentworth, England	Dale Hayes (SA)	lost second round	£2,000
Spanish Open	El Prat, Barcelona	Brian Barnes (GB)	J-5	£1,089
Tournament of Champions	La Costa, California	Gary Player (SA)	J-7	$7,389
Sun Alliance European Match Play	Dalmahoy, Scotland	Mark James (GB)	7	£1,400
World Series of Golf	Firestone, Ohio	Gill Morgan (US)	J-9	$6,450
Dunlop Phoenix	Phoenix, Miyazaki, Japan	Andy Bean (US)	J-11	Y1,038,571
US Open	Cherry Hills, Denver	Andy North (US)	J-16	$2,650
British Open	St Andrews, Scotland	Jack Nicklaus (US)	J-17	£1,600

EVENT	SITE	WINNER	BALLESTEROS	PRIZE MONEY
US Masters	Augusta National, Georgia	Gary Player (SA)	J-18	$2,550
PGA championship (GB)	Royal Birkdale, England	Nick Faldo (GB)	J-36	£335
Memphis Classic	Colonial, Tenn.	Andy Bean (US)	J-39	$1,025
European Open	Walton Heath, England	Bobby Wadkins (US)	missed cut	£270
Hennessy Cup	The Belfry, England	Great Britain and Ireland beat Europe	won two singles halved one singles lost one singles halved one foursomes	

British Order of Merit   First

DOMESTIC				
Spanish Under-25 Professional championship	Torrequebrada, Torremolinos	Ballesteros	—	Ptas 50,000

1 9 7 9

INTERNATIONAL				
British Open	Royal Lytham and St Annes, England	Ballesteros	—	£15,000
English Golf Classic	The Belfry, England	Ballesteros	—	£8,330
Scandinavian Enterprises Open	Vasatorps, Sweden	Sandy Lyle (GB)	2	£3,530
French Open	Lyon	Bernard Gallacher (GB)	J-3	£2,008
Western Australian Open	Lake Karrinyup, Perth	Peter Jacobsen (US)	J-3	A$7,575
Suntory World Match Play championship	Wentworth, England	Bill Rogers (US)	beaten in semi-final	£9,500
Italian Open	Como	Brian Barnes (GB)	J-5	£1,110
European Open	Turnberry, Scotland	Sandy Lyle (GB)	J-6	£2,233
Japan Open	Hino, Gamo	Kuo Chie-Hsiung (Tai)	J-7	$6,000
Australian Open	Metropolitan, Melbourne	Jack Newton (Aus)	8	A$4,200
Martini International	Wentworth, England	Greg Norman (Aus)	J-7	£1,155
Madrid Open	Puerta de Hierro	Simon Hobday (Zim)	J-9	£662
PGA championship (GB)	St Andrews, Scotland	Vicente Fernandez (Arg)	J-10	£870
Greater Greensboro Open	Greensboro, NC	Ray Floyd (US)	J-12	£4,750
US Masters	Augusta National	Fuzzy Zoeller (US)	J-12	$3,740
German Open	Frankfurt	Tony Jacklin (GB)	16	£468
Carrols Irish Open	Portmarnock, Dublin	Mark James (GB)	J-17	£760
Dunlop Masters	Woburn, England	Graham Marsh (Aus)	J-25	£690
Benson and Hedges	St Mellion, England	Maurice Bembridge (GB)	J-57	£210
Tournament Players championship (US)	Sawgrass, Fla.	Lanny Wadkins (US)	missed cut	
US Open championship	Inverness, Toledo	Hale Irwin (US)	missed cut	
Ryder Cup	White Sulphur Springs, W. Va.	US beat Europe	lost one singles, lost two fourballs, lost one foursome, won one foursome	

DOMESTIC				
El Prat Open	El Prat, Barcelona	Ballesteros	—	Ptas 250,000
Catalunian Professionals championship	San Cugat, Barcelona	Jose-Maria Canizares	2	Ptas 60,000

British Order of Merit Finish 2   (winner—Sandy Lyle GB)

EVENT	SITE	WINNER	BALLESTEROS	PRIZE MONEY
1980				
INTERNATIONAL				
US Masters	Augusta National	Ballesteros	—	$55,000
Madrid Open	Puerta de Hierro, Madrid	Ballesteros	—	£5,118
Martini International	Wentworth, England	Ballesteros	—	£9,000
Dutch Open	Hilversum	Ballesteros	—	£5,495
Australian PGA	Melbourne GC	Sam Torrance (GB)	2	A$15,000
Gene Sarazen Jun Classic	Jun Classic CC, Tochigi	Isao Aoki (Jap)	2	Y3,500,000
Spanish Open	Escorpian GC, Valencia	Eddie Polland (GB)	J-2	£3,645
Bob Hope British Classic	RAC Golf and CC	Jose-Maria Canizares (Sp)	J-2	£6,690
Dunlop Phoenix	Phoenix CC, Miyazaki	Tom Watson (US)	3	Y4,500,000
Tournament Players Championship (US)	Sawgrass, Ponte Vedra Beach, Florida	Lee Trevino (US)	J-3	$23,200
Scandinavian Enterprises Open	Vasatorps GC, Helsingborg, Sweden	Greg Norman (Aus)	J-3	£2,591
Carrolls Irish Open	Portmarnock GC, Dublin	Mark James (GB)	4	£3,580
Johnnie Walker Trophy	El Prat GC, Barcelona, Spain	Lee Trevino (US)	4	$3,000
Lancome Trophy	St-Nom-La-Breteche, Paris	Lee Trevino (US)	J-5	£1,141
Suntory World Match Play	Wentworth, England	Greg Norman (Aus)	Lost, second round	£5,000
Tournament Players' Championship (GB)	Moortown GC, Leeds	Bernard Gallacher (GB)	J-7	£1,600
German Open	Berlin G and CC, Wannsee	Mark McNulty (SA)	J-8	£996
Colombian Open	Bogota CC	Bernard Langer (Ger)	15	$750
Australian Open	The Lakes GC, Sydney	Greg Norman (Aus)	J-11	A$3,465
Jackie Gleason Inverrary Classic (US)	Inverrary G and CC, Lauderdale, Florida	Johnny Miller (US)	J-15	$4,800
Tournament of Champions	La Costa, California	Tom Watson (US)	J-18	$4,917
British Open	Muirfield, Scotland	Tom Watson (US)	J-19	£2,013
European Open	Walton Heath GC, Tadworth	Tom Kite (US)	J-31	£690
Sun Alliance PGA championship	Royal St George's, Sandwich, England	Nick Faldo (GB)	J-32	£550
Benson and Hedges International	Fulford GC, York	Graham Marsh (Aus)	J-42	£452
Hennessy Cup	Sunningdale GC, England	Gt Britain and Ireland bt Europe	won one singles, lost one singles, lost one foursomes, lost one fourball	£2,000
Doral Eastern Open	Doral CC, Miami, Fla.	Ray Floyd (US)	missed cut	
US Open	Baltusrol GC, Springfield, NJ	Jack Nicklaus (US)	disqualified	
British Order of Merit 3	*(winner—Sandy Lyle GB)*			
1981				
INTERNATIONAL				
Scandinavian Enterprises Open	Lidkoping	Ballesteros	—	£8,330
Spanish Open	El Prat, Barcelona	Ballesteros	—	£8,571
Suntory World Match Play championship	Wentworth, England	Ballesteros	—	£30,000
Australian PGA	Royal Melbourne	Ballesteros	—	£17,000
Dunlop Phoenix	Phoenix, Miyazaki, Japan	Ballesteros	—	£26,840
Million Dollar Challenge	Sun City, Bophuthatswana, SA	Johnny Miller (US)	2	$160,000
European Open	Royal Liverpool, England	Graham Marsh (Aus)	2	£11,500
Sanyo Open	San Cugat, Barcelona	Bernard Gallacher (GB)	2	Ptas 200,000
Tournament Players' Championship (GB)	Dalmahoy, Scotland	Brian Barnes (GB)	J-3	£3,100
French Open	St Germain, Paris	Sandy Lyle (GB)	J-3	£2,115
Johnnie Walker Trophy	La Moraleja, Madrid	Peter Jacobsen (US)	J-3	£5,400

EVENT	SITE	WINNER	BALLESTEROS	PRIZE MONEY
Dunlop International (Japan)	Ibaragi, Tokyo	Kohsaku Shimada (Jap)	J-5	£4,625
Chunichi Crowns	Wago, Nagoya	Graham Marsh (Aus)	J-7	Y1,750,000
Bob Hope British Classic	Moor Park, England	Bernard Langer (Ger)	J-22	£948
Heritage Classic	Hilton Head, SC	Bill Rogers (US)	J-25	$2,450
Tournament Players' Championship (US)	Sawgrass, Fla.	Lee Trevino (US)	J-29	$2,600
US Open	Merion, Pa.	David Graham (Aus)	J-41	$1,570
Greater Greensboro Open	Greensboro, NC	Larry Nelson (US)	J-45	$826
Doral Eastern Open	Doral, Miami	Ray Floyd (US)	J-50	$603
US Masters	Augusta National	Tom Watson (US)	missed cut	
British Order of Merit Finish 7	*(winner—Bernard Langer, Ger)*			

ACKNOWLEDGMENTS

The authors wish to thank these people, together with scores who deserve equal gratitude, who have helped us with this book: Cyril Gregory of Royal Lytham and St Annes, Colin Maclaine, John Behrend and others in the Royal and Ancient Golf Club of St Andrews, Peter Ryde of *The Times*, Jorge de Ceballos, Jesus Ruiz and Mercedes Santa-Maria, Enid Watson, Dave Musgrove, our colleagues on the course and in the press tent and, most of all, the Ballesteros family who gave generously of their time.

INDEX

155